The Football Industry

The Football Industry

by Peter Douglas

London George Allen & Unwin Ltd
Ruskin House Museum Street

First published in 1973

ISBN ⬤ 04 796041 8

Printed in Great Britain
in 11 point Plantin type
by Clarke, Doble & Brendon Ltd
Plymouth

*For Barry Walsh and
Russell Thomas,
two football experts*

Preface

This book is a very personal examination of professional football in England. In the course of researching and writing, the problem has been not what to include but what had to be left out. Inevitably there will be gaps.

The book, too, is written entirely from a layman's point of view. Although I have been a professional journalist for a number of years, I have never been called upon to write a match commentary nor had the privilege of travelling with players at a newspaper's expense.

All the information contained in this book comes from published sources, in particular the Chester Report, newspaper and magazine articles, and from personal contact with footballers. The conclusions drawn are entirely my own.

I have very much enjoyed contact with the players and personalities I have met in the game and I hope that I have been able to do them justice. I hope too that this book will provide enlightenment and some entertainment, debunk a few myths and expose a number of wrongs.

And, above all, set professional football in its context as one of the most interesting social phenomena of our times.

Contents

Chapter 1

Football Economics

Any weekend during the football season in Great Britain, about a million people will be playing football – and close on a million will be watching the professional game. That is the size of the industry.

Those playing will range from the thousand-odd super-fit players who make up the staffs of the ninety-two Football League clubs over four Divisions, through minor professional, semi-pro and amateur leagues, right down to youth and schoolboy football and countless kick-around games in public parks and on village greens.

In spite of all this activity, however, it is the top professional games that attract most attention, and of those the twenty-two clubs in the First Division of the Football League will attract more spectators than the totals of the other three Divisions put together. The rich clubs get richer, and the small clubs stay small, or get smaller. These are the harsh facts of football life.

Every aspect of the top-level professional game is geared towards a handful of First Division clubs: they attract most attention from television, radio and the national press; their players are the highest paid, raised to superstar status by their comparatively new-found wealth and fan magazine worship; their movements from club to club command high fees in transfer deals; and European football brings more cash and more glamour still to these top clubs. How rich clubs get richer and how the poor survive we shall look at in greater detail.

THE FOOTBALL LEAGUE

The Football League (England) is just one of forty groups of clubs operating in the British Isles. These leagues include the Scottish League, and more or less powerful minor leagues like the Football Combination, Isthmian League, and Northern Premier, which all control and organize football at various levels of the game, under the overall supervision of the national body, the Foorball Association.

The Football League was formed in 1888 with twelve members but today numbers ninety-two professional football clubs, divided into four Divisions. The First and Second Divisions each have twenty-two clubs, and there are twenty-four clubs each in Divisions Three and Four. Each club plays the other twice during the football season, and the results, based on a points system, determine the club's League placing inside its particular Division.

The top club in the First Division becomes Football League Champion – Liverpool won this honour at the end of season 1972-3 with sixty points from forty-two games. Arsenal were close on their heels with fifty-seven, and behind them Leeds United with fifty-three.

In the other Divisions, being at the top means promotion to a higher Division, while failure results in relegation, which is also the fate of the bottom three clubs in Division One. They go down to the Second, and three clubs come up to replace them. Three clubs also come up from the Third Division, while the bottom four go down to the Fourth (and four come up). At the lowest end, the four bottom clubs of the Fourth Division have to apply for re-election at the annual general meeting of the League.

This reshuffle at the end of the season can lead to clubs leaving the Football League, and in June 1972 Barrow lost, and their place was taken by Southern Leaguers Hereford United. The three other clubs – Northampton Town, Crewe Alexandra and Stockport – were re-elected. Tiny Hereford hit the headlines during the 1971-2 season when they reached the fourth round of the FA Cup, knocking out Newcastle United on the way, and holding West Ham to a 0–0 draw before being beaten 3–1 in the replay, at Upton Park.

Success in the League carries with it an even greater prize – entry into European football. The League champions can enter for the European Champions' Cup, while the First Division's runners-up in second and third place can enter for the Inter Cities Fairs Cup.

In addition to the League programme, and, for some clubs, European competitions, there are two main domestic competitions, the FA Cup and the Football League Cup, both culminating in a final at Wembley Stadium. There are also sponsored competitions, like the Watney Cup, and Texaco Cup financed by brewerery and petroleum interests respectively.

All this means that a successful club can face fifty or sixty top-level games in a season which is already extended to forty or more weeks of the year. This means extra cash at the turnstiles but extra strain on individual players, who may be called upon to play for their countries as well, or summoned for England Under-23 duty.

WHERE THE MONEY COMES FROM

The more successful a club, the greater will be its gate receipts, and it is only lower down the scale that clubs have to rely for survival on extra-curricula activities like pools and bingo and the supporters' club. There is of course income from transfer fees, but as we shall see this too favours the larger, already successful clubs. The League and the Football Association also distribute money, but this is little more than a lifeline to struggling clubs.

Balancing gate receipts against operating costs is the perennial problem of any football club, and the pattern over the last twenty-five years has been one of declining attendances and rising costs. This is not a healthy situation and it is one that does not appear to receive the attention it should from those concerned with the survival of the game. The boom in leisure activities and the advent of the four-day working week should provide sources of new interest in spectator sports, but these, as we shall see, are simply not being catered for by football's administrators.

Taking a broad view, attendances at football matches have shown, apart from a slight rise in season 1967–8, a steady decline since the end of the war. The height of the boom was in 1948–9 with just over 41 million spectators, at a time when even motorcycle speedway was pulling in fifty thousand-plus crowds at Wembley Stadium. Thereafter a gradual decline set in, so that by 1965-6 attendances had dropped by over a quarter and gates reached an all-time low of just under 29 million.

The World Cup helped boost figures a little in 1966-7 and the rise continued – 30 million the following year. Since then however, attendances have dropped again and season 1971–2 resulted in 28,700,729 spectators passing through the turnstiles. This is a little above the average for pre-war dates, demonstrating that nothing has been done to increase the interest in football in a quarter of a century.

In the rise and fall of attendances, the First Division has fared worst, attracting some 18 millions in the immediate post-war years and then dropping to an all-time low in 1961–2 with 12 million. This fall has been arrested and figures for 1971–2 show a rise to just under 14½ million.

The Second Division's decline was even more dramatic, with nearly half of its 1947–8 peak of 12¼ million being lost by 1966–7. This figure has stayed more or less constant, except for a further decline in 1971–2 to 6,769,308.

There were similar falls in the Third and Fourth Divisions, but there, unfortunately, the decline has not been arrested. What is more significant is that it is the top clubs that can boost their attendances with successful runs in the FA and League Cup and European competitions, with the result that the attendance at First Division League games still exceeds the totals of attendances in Divisions Two, Three and Four.

What this means to the lowlier clubs is that attendances rarely reach 10,000 per game, and many clubs average around 3,000. So that in a whole season their total attendances do not exceed the number of spectators at one top First Division game! In 1966–7 Rochdale's total for the season was just over 56,000 – less than the ground capacity of many First Division clubs.

CASH RECEIPTS

In spite of rising costs, football is still a relatively cheap form of entertainment. It has been argued, usually by football authorities, that we enjoy the cheapest football in Europe. This is not strictly true, as wages and therefore prices are higher in most continental countries and any comparison of admission prices must be made in relation to these differentials.

Admission prices have risen since the popular 1s before the war. This became 2s by 1950 and 3s ten years later. Another decade passed and we saw the minimum rise to 4s 6d or 5s, and at the League's annual meeting on 2 June 1972 the minimum admission price was further increased from 30p to 40p.

One can argue whether an overall standard minimum charge is a good thing, when, faced with a choice between a First Division game or a match in the Second or Third, a football fan may decide to spend his 40p to get top-class football, and help to swell the gates of a First Division club.

These increases have done something to cushion the effect of falling attendances, though other factors have operated: the value of money has fallen and operating expenses, notably players' wages since 1961, have increased. The Chester Report* has some interesting figures.

The largest increases have again been in Division One, where match receipts rose 72 per cent between 1956 and 1966; in the Second Division the rise was far less spectacular, a mere 15 per cent for the same period. Operating costs however rose by

---

* The Chester Report was published in 1968 and was the result of an enquiry into football under the chairmanship of Norman Chester, Warden of Nuffield College, Oxford. The committee was appointed in June 1966 by the Department of Education and Science, 'to enquire into the state of Association Football at all levels, including the organization, management, finance and administration and the means by which the game may be developed for the public good; and to make recommendations'.
Unfortunately most of the findings have been ignored.

almost the same amount in the two Divisions – by a staggering 157 per cent in the First and by 131 per cent in the Second.

The one factor most responsible for the increase in costs was the abolition of the maximum wage agreement in 1961, following a strike by players. During this period (1955–64) all players' wages rose by 160 per cent and those of first team players by 235 per cent, in the First Division. The rises were not quite so sharp in the other Divisions, but overall the figures for all four show an increase of 120 per cent for all players and 148 per cent for first team players. During the corresponding period, industrial earnings rose on average by 62 per cent.

By the mid-sixties, increases in both receipts and expenses had settled down, with the First Division clubs again coming off best. There, receipts rose by 30 per cent against a rise in costs of only 15 per cent. But the other three Divisions all lost, with rises in costs of 22, 14 and 9 per cent against increases in receipts of only 16, 8 and 6 per cent respectively.

The actual figures are given in the Chester Report, and show that only the First Division clubs made a profit (nearly £1½ million between them), and the rest made a loss: £788,000 in the Second Division; and £1½ million in Divisions Three and Four respectively. Overall the ninety-two League clubs lost just under £2½ million between them during the three seasons 1963–4 to 1965–6.

Not all clubs make profits or suffer losses according to which Division they are in: some clubs, usually in a race for promotion, attract enormous gates, or are happily placed with little or no serious opposition. It is the Second and Third Division clubs in too close proximity to London and Lancashire that suffer worst. There are of course exceptions like Aston Villa, newly promoted to the Second Division in 1971–2, whose gates have been known to pass the 50,000 mark, in spite of opposition from nearby Birmingham City, West Bromwich Albion, Leicester and Coventry City. But the overall pattern is one of rich clubs getting richer, and the lowlier clubs struggling along, just making ends meet or losing money every season.

Other sources of income – and these become more important as we go down the Divisions – include fees from the transfer of players, and fund-raising efforts by supporters' clubs which include bingo, sweepstakes and club pools. There are also handouts from the Football Association and the League.

Nearly 90 per cent of all additional revenue comes from fund-raising efforts of this kind: and in the Fourth Division compensates for some two-thirds of the clubs' operating deficits, or a ratio of £1 to every £2 taken at the gate in the Third and Fourth Divisions taken together.

Transfer fees regularly attract large headlines, and the season 1971–2 saw several £200,000 transfers between clubs: Alan Ball (Everton to Arsenal); Rodney Marsh (Queens Park Rangers to Manchester City); Ian Moore (Nottingham Forest to Manchester United) and Martin Peters (West Ham United to Tottenham).

It will be noticed that most of these moves are between clubs in the First Division (apart from Rodney Marsh), so that again there is a continuing trend for the top clubs to spend and receive large sums when it comes to transfer fees. The popular idea that small clubs survive by breeding exciting new players and then selling them to a top club simply does not hold good, and looked at overall (as we shall in chapter 5) transfers work downwards rather than upwards, with players being sold by First Division clubs to clubs in lower Divisions and not vice versa. The other main beneficiaries are clubs in Scotland and Ireland, which sell promising players to English League clubs.

Payments are made to clubs by the Football Association, largely as a result of participating in competitions like the FA Challenge Cup. A percentage of the gate receipts is paid into a pool and then distributed equally to all League clubs, rich or poor. This is clearly a stupid situation, when a payment of some £3,000 or £4,000 could make all the difference between survival and disaster for a Third or Fourth Division club; and yet exactly the same sum is paid out to First Division clubs – equivalent to the basic salary of one of their lesser known players.

The Football League make several kinds of distributions to clubs. These include a percentage of the gate receipts of all

B

matches played in the League Cup; a levy on gate receipts and the total of fees received for televising games; and payments by the Pools Promoters Association for the rights to reproduce the fixtures lists. The total of amounts available for distribution can amount to over a million pounds each season, allowing each club something between £10,000 and £15,000 from the League's funds.

WHAT MAKES FOR SUCCESS OR FAILURE?

There are a number of factors that will make for the success or failure of a football club. But there are also general influences of a more serious kind of work, affecting spectator sports as a whole and not just the football industry. We will look at these in turn.

One of the most important changes in the last decade has been the increase in prosperity generally, and with it the increase in mobility. Families now own cars and take their holidays abroad. Because they are mobile, they can afford to live out of town and further from the catchment areas of many old-established football clubs situated in areas of dense urban population. People tend to take their leisure more seriously, going away at weekends to second homes in the country or taking day outings to the sea.

Young people are freer from parental restrictions and travel further and more often. Young wage earners can afford to spend their money on clothes and entertainment, motorcycles or cars. There has also been a boom in do-it-yourself activities, which tend to tie many husbands to the home on Saturday afternoons. There is also the increasing tendency to do the shopping only once a week, and this means an excursion to the nearby supermarket on Saturday.

The five-day week is now almost universal, bringing with it the prospect of a long weekend of leisure. Television has played a dual role in sports: bringing the best of football and other sports to the small screen, and interesting and exciting an entirely new audience, particularly among women and among the middle classes generally. Conversely, the certainty of being able to watch sport from one's armchair tends to discourage spectators from turning out on a cold or wet Saturday afternoon to watch an indifferent football team.

There is also growing competition from other spectator sports: Lord Wigg worked hard to popularize racing and sell it as something not exclusively for the upper classes; motor racing is gaining in popularity, and speedway has seen a revival, thanks partly to increased television coverage.

There has also been an increase in participation rather than just watching: fishing is the greatest participatory sport in the country and young people especially are drawn to playing football, camping, cycling, canoeing. Tennis and squash are increasing in popularity, and golf has ceased to be a game for bank managers.

Rising standards of comfort and prosperity mean that the modern generation is more critical of facilities generally, and to cater for their more sophisticated tastes brand-new bowling alleys have been constructed or cinemas and theatres refurbished. By contrast, it is only comparatively recently that football clubs have turned their attention to making ground improvements.

Several London clubs have added new stands over the last decade, and Chelsea have drawn up plans for an ambitious new development at their Stamford Bridge ground. But many clubs are hampered by inaccessibility, so that car parking is a nightmare, and simply have no room to expand, hemmed in by houses or factories or – in the case of Fulham – by the river Thames.

Women in particular will not be attracted to football grounds until the standard of toilet accommodation has improved. Catering, too, has lagged behind other forms of entertainment and at most grounds it is simply not worth the trouble to try to get a cup of tea or a sandwich at half-time unless you find yourself placed close to one of the tea bars. Often these are depressing and unhygienic and service is painfully slow.

There is also the problem of misbehaviour among spectators. It is true that stories of crowd violence tend to get blown up by a sensation-hungry press, but the effect is to put people off whether these accounts are exaggerated or not. Most of the culprits are youngsters scarcely into their teens and in any crowd of 50,000 there is bound to be a certain amount of pushing and shoving given the bad conditions on the terraces.

Police surveillance has been stepped up and stiffer penalties are now imposed by magistrates. Clubs are fined by the League for crowd misbehaviour (a curious situation indeed), and appeals to the fans are printed in football programmes. There is also the sheer difficulty of getting to some football grounds: press reports of wrecked supporters' trains and the damage regularly done to the London Underground are scarcely likely to encourage wavering supporters.

Once inside the ground, unless you arrive an hour or more beforehand, it is often impossible to secure a good vantage point at any First Division club from the open terracing. Seats for important matches are sold out well beforehand and season ticket holders are increasing. This might seen like a healthy sign, except that with a choice of clubs to watch as in London, the Midlands or Lancashire, it is clearly prohibitive to subscribe to a season ticket at every club; and the fag of trying to buy a ticket for a particular game would discourage all but the stoutest supporter.

The computer booking revolution seems to have by-passed the football industry, almost entirely. At a time when you can inevitably get a seat for your local cinema or pick up the telephone to book a theatre seat or even a Wembley spectacular, buying tickets for a football match invariably means two journeys to the ground and a long queue at an under-staffed ticket office.

Nothing is being done by the industry to sell football to the new prosperous leisured classes. Football matches are almost never advertised: Queens Park Rangers actually bought television time on Thames in February 1972 to advertise a friendly match with West Bromwich Albion. Unless you are already a sports fan, matches are not listed until the morning of the day they are due to be played, and for this you have to scan the sports pages of the national press. You might think it impossible to be unaware of the start of the new football season in August, yet a quick poll among colleagues and friends can reveal a surprising lack of knowledge of this event.

Even if you are a football fan, the days of blind loyalty to a particular team are passing and increased mobility means that spectators can shop around in some areas for the best football entertainment available. This is particularly true of football clubs situated in large centres of population: London has currently five First Division clubs (Arsenal, Chelsea, Queens Park Rangers, Tottenham and West Ham); four in the Second Division (Fulham, Millwall, Orient and Crystal Palace) plus Luton in the suburbs; one Third Division club (newly relegated Charlton) and one, Brentford, in the Fourth. Watford, just north of London, is now in the Third Division.

But it is in the north of England and particularly Lancashire that you find football's traditional strongholds, Manchester and Liverpool each supporting two First Division teams, and a host of secondary clubs fall within their shadows, including Burnley, Blackpool, Preston, Huddersfield, Bolton, Blackburn, Oldham, Tranmere, Rochdale, Rotherham, Stockport, Bury and Barnsley.

The Midlands, the North-East and Yorkshire also support several First Division clubs between them. Occasionally, away from these centres you find a prosperous club (no matter what Division), usually because there is no opposition for miles around. Ipswich, for example, more than holds its own in the First Division, while Southampton struggles. Norwich, of all teams, gained promotion to the First Division at the end of the 1971-2 season, and for many years Burnley, almost isolated in northern Lancashire, has been known as the enigma of the First Division.

The fortunes of clubs rise and fall and this affects gates: many Londoners have watched Fulham playing in Divisions One, Two and Three over the last five years, and the 1971-2 season saw the phenomenal progress of Aston Villa into the Second Division, and of Birmingham City into the First. A Midlands revival certainly.

But it is the top ten or so clubs that consistently attract

support, with Liverpool alone pulling in over a million specta-tors during the season 1972–3.

Playing success is only a partial guarantee of support, and for some reason even Leeds United do not always attract big gates. Whereas Coventry, always good at public relations but indifferent on the field of play, have attracted publicity and support through the personality of managers like Jimmy Hill, Noel Cantwell, and now ex-Manchester City patriarch Joe Mercer.

Some clubs seem almost to go out of their way to alienate supporters in their carefree attitude to fans: Queens Park Rangers, flushed with the prospects of elevation into the First Division in 1968, upset fans by throwing up a hastily con-structed stand and selling off season tickets, only to find that the structure was not ready by the start of the new season. When the club was back down in Division Two, it stood as a chastening reminder of dashed hopes and thwarted ambitions.

Crystal Palace are another mystery. Thanks to former manager Bert Head's forays into the Scottish footballing scene he has managed to gather round him a hotch-potch of 'Anglos' from obscure Scottish clubs like Kilmarnock and Stenhousemuir. This sort of propping-up operation is hardly calculated to engender *local* support among south Londoners.

Fulham is a distinctly unfriendly club, with the supporters' club regularly calling for the resignation of chairman Tommy Trinder and a lack of star names in their first team line-up. Perhaps aware of their tarnished image, Fulham in February 1973 hired the services of former Coventry manager and television pundit Jimmy Hill to launch a major public relations exercise for the club.

When a First Division club needs regular gates of 25–35,000 and Second Division clubs maybe 10,000 less, it is surprising that so little attention is paid to elementary public relations by the industry. Falling attendances start off a vicious spiral, with little or no money being forthcoming for the purchase of 'name' players or making improvements to the ground. It is argued in some quarters that supporters will turn out in any sort of conditions to cheer a winning side: but in these days of increasingly sophisticated leisure this is becoming less and less true, and team-building and ground improvements simply must go hand in hand.

There were three main proposals put forward in the Chester Report which are worthy of attention, and which would go a long way to revamping football in the seventies – a decade when expenditure on leisure is estimated to be doubling.* They are: Sunday football; summer football; and the sharing of ground facilities.

SUNDAY FOOTBALL

The playing of matches on a Saturday afternoon was a good idea when most of us worked a five-and-a-half-day week. Spectators clocked off, managed to grab a pint of beer and a sandwich at the local pub, and then went on in their working clothes to the afternoon match. It was this pattern that did much to contribute to football's cloth-cap image.

Nowadays, with the almost universal five-day week and the prospects of a four-day week and a three-day weekend, clearly Saturday afternoon – right in the middle of the break – is not a good time for staging football matches. A much more suitable time would be Friday evening (under floodlighting if necessary) or late Sunday afternoon or evening.

There are always objections to the so-called Continental Sunday, condemning the British to a drab holiday, with indifferent public transport, and restaurants closed and public houses limited to the frantic lunch-time drink hours and the curtailed evening session.

Usually the objections are on religious grounds, and come from vociferous minority groups like the Lord's Day Observance Society. The comparison with the Continent is amusing, as in countries like France, Spain and Italy which all stage Sunday sport there is a far greater proportion of religious observance, if one measures this by attendance at church, than there is in Great Britain. Clearly, religion and enjoyment are not

* W. Beckerman, *The British Economy in 1975* (Cambridge University Press, 1965), p. 197.

incompatible and it is only among older people that strict observance of the Lord's Day is a hardened custom.

Inevitably, we are moving towards the four-day working week, which will bring with it the three-day weekend*. What this means is that vast new leisure *industries* will have to be created, to cater for this extended amount of free time, and some will be obliged to work while others take their leisure. This is the case now when shops remain open all day Saturday to cater for the five-day working-week customers, while shop assistants put in an eight-hour stint to cater for them.

Leisure hours will of course have to be staggered, as obviously not everyone can take their leisure at once, otherwise the country would come to a standstill. Public transport will clearly have to be improved, if the majority are to enjoy and take advantage of a longer weekend, and additional staff will be required in catering, parks and pleasure gardens – and sports grounds.

As has been pointed out, already more and more people are travelling away at weekends to second homes or the coast; and Saturday is increasingly a day of shopping or household activities. Clearly, football played late on Sunday afternoon would attract more spectators, as this is the time of the notorious hiatus in the weekend's activities. Sunday evening football would provide a pleasant end to the weekend and would not interfere with other planned activities.

SUMMER FOOTBALL

The case for summer football is even stronger. Football is only by tradition a winter game, leaving the summer free for cricket – a sport with dwindling support. The 1966 World Cup was played in England in July and demonstrated to millions that summer football is enjoyable.

There are no convincing arguments against summer football. Already the League programme is overcrowded, so that the close season is only a matter of a few weeks between the end of May and the beginning of August. Often pitches get water-

* Riva Poor (ed.), *Four Days, Forty Hours* (Pan Books).

logged or frozen-over in mid-winter, and rain and freezing cold conditions are not the best in which to watch from the terraces for an hour and a half.

The only main change would be that players and managers would have to take their holidays in mid-winter, if the season ran from, say, mid-February to mid-November, leaving the two worst months in terms of weather (December and January) free. More and more players are taking their holidays abroad, so that a mid-winter break would probably suit them. Grounds that take a pounding in snow and slush would have a chance to recover, and the notorious fair-weather supporter would be encouraged to turn out more often to watch the club of his choice.

GROUND CHANGES

The third change that must come is a drastic improvement in ground facilities, and with that the sharing of grounds. It is inconceivable that cities like Liverpool, Manchester, Bristol or Nottingham should try to support two large clubs – huge areas of expensive ground, ripe for development, and yet used only on alternate Saturdays.

The sale of, for example, the two Manchester grounds could lead to a massive investment in a purpose-built sports centre which would be shared by the two First Division clubs. This arrangement can work – both Munich clubs share the same ground, and three clubs have combined to build the new stadium in Mexico City.

There are arguments that clubs could lose their identity, but this could be overcome by building their own headquarters housing administrative offices and supporters' club in a central location. This would have the effect of bringing the football club into the city, when at present grounds are usually inaccessible. The public relations value would be enormous and ticket sales could be conducted from a central box office.

The Munich stadium belongs to the local authority, which then rents it to the clubs in return for a share (usually 10 or 15 per cent) of gate receipts. At a time of concern about crowd safety, and cries from clubs that they could not afford to carry out the improvements recommended in the Wheatley Report, it seems logical to involve the local authority, and with it the local community, in building a purpose-built stadium, that would be the pride of the townspeople.

Football clubs at present are operating almost outside the law and unlike other entertainment complexes are not subject to inspection and licensing by the local Watch Committee. Accidents and deaths have occurred at grounds in the last few years, when safety barriers have collapsed or grounds have been packed to a dangerous capacity.

The modern spectator demands or will demand better facilities, and a survey undertaken by the League ten years ago showed, fairly obviously, that poor facilities and lack of parking space helped to drive away attenders at matches. More covered seating is required and greater ease of booking in advance. This would encourage more family attendance at matches, while at present only one in ten women go to games, though about one third of all women profess an interest in football. Wives and girl-friends often persuade their menfolk not to go to matches, so that the male spectators can also be lost.

It has also been scientifically demonstrated that less violence occurs when spectators are seated. Easy movement along the terraces, often from one end of the pitch to the other, encourages massing of spectators and leads to violent confrontations between opposing factions. All this could be eliminated by improved facilities.

Clubs are not unaware of the potential wealthy audiences that can be attracted to games, but they invariably go to the extreme of constructing a handful of private Ascot-style boxes, which are invariably snapped up by local businessmen to entertain their friends and clients. This is not solving the problem of the larger mass of reasonably well-to-do, used to and demanding a higher standard of comfort but not necessarily wanting a seat in the directors' enclosure.

Obviously not all towns could afford to embark on such a lavish scheme, but here smaller clubs could be 'adopted' by larger clubs. It is foolish for a wealthy club to pay a hefty corporation tax bill when surplus cash could be channelled into a subsidiary company – a smaller club in a lower division. Clubs do have excess profits, and these are often splashed on the purchase of star players, to such an extent that clubs like Chelsea had players costing £150,000 (Steve Kember) and £100,000 (Chris Garland) playing in the reserves during season 1971–2. Yet clubs of this size also carry enormous staffs of apprentices and argue at the same time that they are developing their youth squads. It would clearly be healthier for the game as a whole if some of this wealth were channelled into football at a lower level.

Finally, as more clubs move into European football and more foreign teams come to play on English soil, we find ourselves having to compete with some of the best facilities in Europe – the stadiums in Munich, Madrid or Lisbon. Even Wembley Stadium is not now large enough for Cup Final events, and there are plans to reduce the capacity to 80,000. Curiously enough London lags behind Glasgow in this respect – the Ibrox Stadium holding no fewer than 120,000 spectators.

Chapter 2

Football Administration

The smallest unit of football administration inside the League is the football club and there are ninety-two of them spread across the four Divisions. With the exception of Nottingham Forest the clubs are limited companies, several of them having been formed as long ago as the turn of the century. The clubs are public companies – that is, the public can buy shares in them, and they are run by a chairman and board of directors.

THE DIRECTORS

What strikes one immediately on studying the balance sheet of almost any football club is the small amount of *share capital* – usually around £10,000 a club – when *turnover* can exceed the half-million mark. Of course, directors loan money to clubs, but one manager remarked bitterly that in his club the qualification for a directorship was the purchase of only fifty shares, and for the investment of a comparatively small sum, a director was guaranteed the best seats, travel to away games and almost limitless hospitality in the boardroom. 'The man drank more than he invested' was the bitter conclusion.

Some clubs are known for their 'personality' chairmen, and names that spring to mind include Arthur Wait of Crystal Palace, Brian Mears of Chelsea and Manny Cussins of Leeds. Hull City is dominated by members of the Needler family, and Burnley is as famous for chairman Bob Lord's pies as it is for its football.

Occasionally there are boardroom battles, and the start of the 1972–3 season saw the resignation of a Crystal Palace director and later the Chairman, and unseemly squabbles at Aston Villa which marred the opening of their first season newly promoted to the Second Division.

Directors appear to acquire their seats on the board through the old-boy network: certainly there is some prestige that goes with the job and you are always sure of a seat. Directors can entertain their friends and business associates at matches, and the sight of the players waiting impatiently in the team coach while the directors are dragged from the boardroom is an all too common sight at away matches.

The Football Association rules forbid the paying of directors' fees, yet there is no restriction in Scotland. The Chester Committee concluded that this was neither a bad nor a good thing, yet it is disturbing to think of a business with a turnover the size of any average First Division club being run by a part-time, unpaid board. The only parallel is the administration of local authority affairs by part-time councillors, but there the motives are, one hopes, altruistic; in the commercial world there is certainly no equivalent.

What is lacking in football management at boardroom level is expertise in financial and administrative areas, skill in personnel management and a knowledge of basic public relations. A love of football and lifelong support for a particular club should not be the only requirements for a seat on the board.

THE SECRETARY

The one person on whom most of the administrative burden falls is the full-time paid club secretary, who is sometimes elevated in name at least to the role of general manager. The average club secretary is a harassed individual, who copes with problems as diverse as the employment of turnstile staff on Saturday afternoon to juggling the club finances and preparing a statement for the monthly board meeting. Many of them get involved in writing the club programme as well.

Club secretaries are an anonymous bunch, and invariably, it

seems, unfriendly and unapproachable people. This is the view of a number of players with whom I spoke. Players have dealings with the secretary usually on the question of wages and when negotiating the terms of their contracts.

THE MANAGER

Further down the scale, and not quite making it to boardroom level, we find the club manager. The manager's personality will shape a club and it is hard in this context to think of Derby County without Brian Clough, or Leeds United without Don Revie. Clough and Revie, together with Bill Shankly of Liverpool, and Malcolm Allison of Crystal Palace, form a sort of soccer elite. They are all ex-players, tough, outspoken and appear frequently on television and in the press with uncompromising pronouncements on almost every aspect of the game. They are track-suit managers, personally involved with and responsible for the welfare and success of their players.

The super-elite are followed by a stream of second-string managers, names that do not as readily come to mind. They include Dave Sexton of Chelsea, Bertie Mee of Arsenal, Ron Greenwood of West Ham, Bill Nicholson of Spurs, and several others.

Managers are notoriously insecure in their jobs, and the strains they undergo were discussed and analysed in the national press at the end of the 1971–2 season. Wives complained of pressures – from directors, from the fans – and almost all predictably enough admitted that if the team was winning they were happy, if not they got depressed.

They were talking of pressures at the top: lower down the Divisions the insecurity is often more basic – fear of losing the job. *Goal* magazine analysed the situation in November 1971, pointing out that the average rate for sackings over the last twenty-five years was one every two weeks (a grand total of 750). Third and Fourth Division managers fare worst, with clubs changing their managers at least once every four years. In the Third Division, Jimmy McGuigan of Chesterfield holds the record at the time of writing – just five years in the job, when all the other clubs have had at least one managerial change in the same period. The record in the Fourth Division belonged to Ron Ashman (five years) and he took the club successfully into Division Three at the end of the 1971–2 season.

The track-suit manager will make himself responsible for the training and tactics of his first team squad. This will involve training sessions, usually every morning from around ten o'clock. He then returns to the club, eats a light lunch or often just a sandwich before tackling the day's administrative problems. These can include talking to the press, answering correspondence, discussions with the chairman and secretary, talking on the telephone to other managers about players for sale or wanted. There may be an evening game, particularly during the early part of the season, and if this is an away fixture it will involve travelling with the team the day before or in the early morning. There are the reserves and juniors to watch, match reports to read, reports on promising players to study. Sometimes a manager will do his own scouting, perhaps accompanied by one of the directors and chief coach, and this will involve travelling to matches at other clubs to watch players' performances.

Thursday is traditionally the manager's day off, though the team will train as usual, but there will be no evening games. Friday is a day for light training and if the Saturday fixture is away, the first team squad will leave around lunch time by coach or train and spend Friday night in a hotel. Saturday is the climax of the week. The players take a light lunch around 12 noon, and arrive at the ground about an hour before kick-off.

The return journey starts as quickly as possible after the end of the game: there are trains to catch and team coaches have to make a dash to the nearest station. Supper is eaten on the train, in a mood of elation or despair depending on the afternoon's results. Reporters often accompany the team, so that the manager is still on call to the press, providing news and quotes for Sunday and Monday's newspapers.

Sundays the manager spends with his family, though often he is in touch with the chairman about the team's performance the day before. Players who have received injuries will report to the club on Sunday morning for treatment and the manager may be on hand to assess the situation, particularly if he has another evening fixture on the Monday or Tuesday. And on Monday morning, the whole process starts all over again.

THE COACH

Some managers are rarely seen in a track suit and leave coaching and tactics to the chief coach. He is invariably an ex-player, who may have served with the same club, and who nurses secret longings to be a manager. There is no glory in being a coach: success, if any, reflects on the manager, while failures are invariably blamed on the coach.

Amongst those who have made the transition smoothly from coach to manager are Malcolm Allison, for many years understudy to Joe Mercer at Manchester City; Don Howe who left Arsenal to take over West Bromwich Albion; and George Petchey, former Crystal Palace coach, who moved into management with Orient.

THE TRAINER

Lower down the scale and performing the functions of wet-nurse and general dogsbody is the team trainer – the man who races on to the pitch with a wet sponge when one of his team is injured. The trainer may double as a scout and look after the junior or apprentice squads. He also collects up the players' kit scattered round the shower room after a game and administers everything from advice to sticking plaster to the players. He is generally popular and long-suffering: everybody leans on him.

THE PLAYERS

At the bottom of the hierarchy we find the mere players. I put them at the bottom as many clubs give the impression that they could almost manage without them. If you have been to football matches, you will hear the announcer welcoming the 'directors, officials and players of . . . club' in that order!

We shall be looking at players in detail in another chapter. They are a squad of fit young and not so young men, sometimes with identical haircuts, smart usually casual clothes, and a new car parked near the dressing-room. If the club is large and prosperous, it will have a first team squad of fifteen or twenty players. Some, and generally only a few of them, have grown up with the club, the products of their youth policy, and have made the first team via apprenticeship and junior ranks. Most of the others will have been purchased from other clubs, usually in the same Division, and will be known for their goal-scoring prowess or their value in midfield or the fullback line.

Backing up this squad is the second or reserve team, each member of which is supposedly striving for a place in the first team squad. They will play matches against other reserve teams in one of the regional professional leagues. After them come the juniors and apprentices, possibly making up a third team squad.

Large clubs can afford to maintain large staffs and often carry professional staffs of fifty or more. Other clubs have enough players to make up a first team with perhaps two or three replacements. Portsmouth currently carries a squad of eighteen players, Mansfield have sixteen, Millwall eighteen. Chelsea carry thirty first-team players, Leeds United have thirty, Manchester City have twenty-nine, Manchester United thirty-four, West Ham twenty-nine, Crystal Palace thirty-five. Carrying a small squad cuts down overheads – the biggest item in a club's budget is the wages bill – but makes the club vulnerable through injuries and illness.

Press accounts of the life-styles of star players like George Best and Rodney Marsh give the impression that footballers earn a lot of money. This is true of an elite of First Division players, but as one Second Division player put it to me what he collects in basic wages is less than a navvy would earn on a building site.

Since the abolition of the maximum wage rule in 1961 following a strike by footballers, players' wages have as we saw in

Chapter 1 leaped ahead of the national industrial average. In reality, they were doing little more than reflect their true value in an entertainment profession, and even if Alan Ball is guaranteed £10,000 a year by Arsenal (according to his father), it is still short of the £30,000 a year earned by top professionals in tennis or golf.

Some players without being star names are steady earners, thanks to long-service bonuses paid out by some clubs. It was this system of payments that angered Arsenal starlet Charlie George at the start of the 1972–3 season when he declared himself unhappy with his financial position and slapped in a transfer request.

Playing life is tending to start earlier – Sammy McIlroy (Manchester United), Willie Donachie (Manchester City), Trevor Francis (Birmingham City) are still youngsters and established players, trailing ten years or more behind players like Francis Lee, Geoff Hurst or Bobby Moore.

At thirty players are veterans by today's standards, though George Eastham (Stoke) and Jackie Charlton (Leeds) played when over thirty-five.

The abolition of the maximum wage has tended to cut down playing staffs by about a fifth, and increase the number of apprentices signed to clubs. The decline was less marked in the Third and Fourth Divisions, partly because they were carrying the minimum staffs anyway, and could not afford to maintain reserve and junior squads. Their wages bills were however still high – in the Fourth Division nearly half that of the First, against receipts of less than a fifth.

SHAREHOLDERS

Another important element in the make-up of a football club is the mass of shareholders. The 'mass' is however often quite small, a situation that was analysed in the Chester Report. In one Second Division club, for example, it was found that half the shares were held by the chairman and the remainder distributed among six other directors. In this situation, provided the directors were in agreement, they could not be voted off the board, there being no other shareholders. At the other extreme, four clubs have over 2,500 shareholders. On average however, clubs had around 500 to 800 shareholders, and bearing in mind that the average share capital of football clubs is usually as low as £10,000, this means that individual shareholdings can amount to £10 or less.

In no fewer than twenty-two clubs, the chairman and directors held more than 50 per cent of the shares, thus again ensuring that their position was secured.

Nottingham Forest is the only exception to the rule and is run as a membership club, not a limited company. Membership is limited to 250 people, who paid just over £1 a year and there is a nine-man management committee, two of whom come up for election each year. Committee members sign personal guarantees to cover the club's commitments, which must effectively reduce active membership to the fairly wealthy as in a limited company set-up. There is however a waiting list for membership.

The Football Association restricts dividends to 7½ per cent per annum and the Chester Committee suggested that this could be raised to bring it into line with normal commercial interest rates and help attract much-needed capital for investment in ground improvements. They also pointed out that raising more capital and increasing thereby the number of shareholders would prevent clubs coming under the control of a handful of individuals.

SUPPORTERS' CLUB

Alongside the shareholders and enjoying a happy or sometimes uneasy relationship with the board are the members of the supporters' club. They may or may not be shareholders (and therefore entitled to vote and voice an opinion) and they have tenuous links with the chairman or a member of the board. In one club I found that the chairman's brother-in-law controlled the supporters' club finances, thus effectively keeping the whole affair in the family.

In lower divisions, the activities of the supporters' club

assume greater importance, with proceeds from whist drives and pools forming an important additional income for the football club.

Managers are at present prevented by the FA rules from becoming board members – under the ruling that board members should receive no remuneration. The Chester Committee recommended that managers should be made an exception to this rule and made members of the board 'to give management its proper status'. Some ex-managers do get on to boards and the elevation of Sir Matt Busby to the board of Manchester United was one of the most recent.

PUBLIC RELATIONS

A figure that has recently made his appearance at some of the more progressive clubs is the PRO or public relations officer. Coventry City were first in the field, and there are PROs at Aston Villa and Reading; Portsmouth have tried, and so have Bolton Wanderers. Leeds United have appointed a public relations team and gimmicks include displays of pre-match exercises by the players, numbered stocking tags and track suits bearing the name of each player.

Although some twenty-five clubs in the League report some effort at improving public relations, few of these are in the top Divisions and it is interesting to note that Arsenal, for example, steadfastly refuse to make any concessions in this direction, in spite of requests by their supporters (during disputes in the 1969–70 season) for 'better public relations'. Unfortunately, too, when someone *is* appointed he is too often a dyed-in-the-wool football journalist, and not a professional public relations man.

As club boards are generally made up of small local businessmen, they are often ignorant of the techniques of public relations and are not at all clear what they are trying to achieve. One professional PR man, who acted as a consultant to a northern Second Division club, complained to me that he got involved in everything from handing out programmes in the press box to checking the bar takings in the supporters' club and booking 'acts' for the following Saturday night. All this for a fee of £1,200 a year!

The model that all clubs try to copy is of course Coventry City. They had a born PR man in Jimmy Hill, who has since made a name for himself as a television personality. It was during Hill's regime that Sky Blue Express supporters' trains were introduced and the standard of football programmes took a dramatic leap forward, and became club magazines.

But it is interesting to note that since their elevation to the First Division in 1967, Coventry have never done really well – they were sixth in 1969–70 – and in spite of massive spending on players and a number of thrusting youngsters in their junior squads, gates started falling at the end of 1971. In November of that year only 16,500 turned up to watch their match against Huddersfield: not enough to keep them going in the Second Division, let alone the First.

Then in March 1972 manager Noel Cantwell left – with a reported £30,000 pay-off – and journalists spent a lot of the close season speculation on his likely successor. Derby's Brian Clough was one of the favourites but in the end young-England manager Gordon Milne was enticed into the job, as team manager, with ex-Manchester City Joe Mercer drafted in as make-weight and elder statesman with the position of general manager. The present first-team squad is home grown, apart from expensive buys like Wilf Smith (£100,000 from Sheffield Wednesday) and Chris Chilton (£92,000 from Hull) and a bargain basement discovery Quinton Young, a Scottish Under-23 cap who cost a mere £30,000.

Coventry have one of the finest grounds in the country – their three-tier stand accommodates a staggering 52,000 spectators, 13,000 of them seated; and the club has an administrative staff of nearly thirty. It will be interesting to watch how they make out in the coming seasons.

PAYING FOR PROGRESS

A typical Second Division club is Preston North End – one of a cluster of clubs too close for comfort to the giants of Manchester and Merseyside. They are buying new players on the instalment plan along the lines of Crystal Palace manager Malcolm Allison's 'rent a player' scheme. They have a supporters' group known as the Phoenix Club and are forming another group known as the Guild Club; membership costs £70 a year, with access to privileged seats and a members' bar. There are 150 members. Schemes like this go part of the way to bridge the gap between the 40p terracing and the luxury boxes of Manchester United and Chelsea.

A fine example of perseverance and dogged faith is newly relegated Brentford, in the Fourth Division. The club has a chequered history. In 1967 they were faced with the possibility of a takeover bid by nearby Queens Park Rangers, when the then chairman Jack Dunnett, MP for Nottingham Central, wished to withdraw his loans to the club, which at the time amounted to some £104,000. The move was firmly resisted by general manager Denis Piggott, who has been associated with the club for over twenty-five years, and a group of directors. Between them they managed to raise the £145,000 needed to pay back the loans and buy Dunnett's shareholding. By dint of economies that involved maintaining a professional staff of just sixteen players, and cutting down on travelling and laundry bills, and powerful fund-raising efforts, they started to pay back the debt, with an indicator outside the club offices showing how the money was coming in. There is a flourishing Bees Club (run by the football club) and a supporters' club. They can get by on gates of 8,000 to 10,000, and in their first year of operation under the new regime showed a profit of £18,500 as against a deficit of £12,500 the year before.

Brentford still have one of the tiniest first-team squads – thirteen at the time of writing!

A Third Division club that has had to fight for survival is Oldham Athletic. Here the situation was not the withdrawal of loan facilities, but the need to recover from the free-spending ways of chairman Ken Bates. Oldham lies in one of soccer's most depressed areas, yet Bates had a vision of a super-club and spent lavishly on providing private viewing boxes, a fully equipped treatment toom, laundry and drying rooms, close-carpeted offices and boardroom, a three-line switchboard and internal intercom system, and some of the most comfortable dressing-rooms in the League, with full central-heating extending over the whole area under the main stand.

Unfortunately, spending on facilities was not matched by success on the field and when Bates retired abroad, the present chairman Harry Massey and a small group of volunteers had to adopt a more realistic approach. With a stadium capable of holding 45,000, the club had to get by for a long time on gates of 4,000 a week. Spending was ruthlessly checked and the directors refused to borrow any more money and get further into debt. Weekly bingo and a golden goal competition bring in fresh funds, and attention has been given to rearing youngsters through an apprentice scheme. The club have a training pitch attached to the main ground and a special drainage system makes it playable all the year round. Reserve games are timed to start an hour before the first team match, so that supporters are encouraged to watch the juniors in action before the big game. They maintain a first-team squad of around twenty, and though they are far from solving all their financial problems, they won promotion into the Third Division in 1971 and ended the 1972–3 season in fourth place.

The efforts of Third and Fourth Division clubs pale somewhat alongside enterprises like the £5 million plan to redevelop Chelsea's ground at Stamford Bridge, Derby's £1 million plans, and Second Division Orient's £750,000 scheme for ground improvements, including a nursery, restaurant, squash courts, gymnasium and space for offices, which would be let. Crystal Palace and Fulham are among the London clubs which have recently built new stands.

Clubs that are lagging behind in spending on ground improvements will have to fall dramatically into line if the government adopts the recommendations of the Wheatley Report on Crowd Safety, which was published in May 1972. The Report was commissioned shortly after the Glasgow Ibrox Stadium disaster, in which sixty-six fans died after the Rangers v. Celtic match on New Year's Day 1971.

The main recommendation of the report was for the compulsory annual licensing of football grounds by the local authority, to bring them in line with other places of public entertainment. The licensing arrangements would be phased over a period of years, but would apply immediately to First and Second Division clubs in Scotland. Uncompromisingly, the Report points out that the cost of providing improvements may force some grounds to close and press estimates at the time of the report put the cost of complying with the recommendations at around £100 million! Even Wembley Stadium, which has a first-class safety record despite attendances of 100,000 for Cup Finals and international games, would fail to comply with the new regulations, as the seats are considered too narrow.

Some clubs would have to reduce their standing accommodation by anything up to 25 per cent, and such a move would cost a club like Liverpool – with a capacity of 54,000 – some £60,000 per season.

The Report was greeted with predictions that admission prices would have to double, to pay for the recommended improvements and the new Value Added Tax. Former sports minister and referee Denis Howell was heading an Opposition motion calling for the exemption of sport from VAT and forecasting a rise in costs of around 30 per cent. Within days, League secretary Alan Hardaker predicted that the minimum admission charge would rise to 50p within a year.

Greatest shock of all was the announcement by the Wembley Stadium management that they were considering reducing the ground capacity to 80,000 – a suggestion that was sharply criticized by J. L. Manning in the *Evening Standard*. As Manning points out, crowds of 100,000 were common at Cup Finals held at the old Crystal Palace at the turn of the century, and the flourishing annual black market in tickets clearly indicates that many more would attend given half a chance. He called for a 150,000 seat stadium and the removal of Wembley from private hands.

Whatever the outcome of the recommendations, it is interesting to note that within two days of the publication of the Report a barrier collapsed at Millwall – not one of soccer's most attractive venues – and eighteen football fans were hurt in the crush during a testimonial match.

Quite apart from improvements on the terraces, little is being done to overcome the problems of waterlogged pitches. There is one artificial all-weather pitch in London's Islington – unattractively situated on a bomb site – and one club at least, Everton, have installed a soil warming system to eliminate ice and slush. Leicester City have gone one better by installing a polythene cover over the entire pitch, so that players can practise in all weather inside a giant air-filled balloon.

Chapter 3

The Government of Football

There are two main bodies concerned with English football – the Football Association and the Football League. Their functions are generally complementary; occasionally they overlap. More recently, the relationship between the two bodies has been one of open war, followed by an uneasy truce.

THE FOOTBALL ASSOCIATION

Every weekend in England, Scotland and Wales some 25,000 games of football are played by some 34,000 clubs, some of which run two or more teams and all of which play in some sort of league. In addition, there are numerous cup, shield and knock-out competitions between clubs, fixture lists have to be prepared, and cup draws made. For every single match a referee has to be provided and a playing pitch allocated. There are often disputes between clubs and breaches of discipline by players, and all these have to be regulated by an official body.

This whole organization is undertaken by volunteers, working through the county sssociations and ultimately coming under the jurisdiction of the Football Association of England, Scotland or Wales. Every club playing in a league or competition is affiliated to the county association, and these vary enormously in size up and down the country. The largest county associations are London and Birmingham, each with 2,500 to 3,000 clubs to administer and not surprisingly the smallest associations are the rural ones; counties like Huntingdon and Westmorland have a hundred or fewer clubs.

The duties of the county associations are many and varied, from recruiting and appointing referees and linesmen, to operating a benevolent fund for players injured while playing football. They also have the job of distributing Cup Final tickets – about one third of the available seats being allocated to the county associations, i.e. around one ticket per member club!

Most of the work is unpaid except for out-of-pocket expenses, which amount to little more than a couple of hundred pounds per year. Some larger associations do have a full-time secretary and impressive new offices, like the Lancashire Association's headquarters opened in January 1972, in Blackburn, complete with council chamber seating 120, and spacious offices. Lancashire look after some 1,500 clubs.

County association revenue is quite small and comes from affiliation fees from every member club and since 1969 the FA has paid some £40,000 a year towards the administrative costs of the county associations. Their turnover is however quite small, often under £2,000 and includes shares of gate money for competitions, referees' affiliation fees, subscriptions and fines paid by players for misconduct. Larger associations have incomes exceeding £10,000 per year, often due to the fact that several professional League clubs are within their catchment area, and contribute substantially from certain matches played.

The Chester Committee expressed concern at the state of the county associations and recommended the appointment of regional offices, to assist in organizing coaching schemes, and developing facilities in the area. The FA countered with estimates of some £125,000 a year which they said would be required to cover clerical assistance, office expenses and the salaries of paid county secretaries. The Chester Committee tactfully reported that they considered the sums 'were guesses rather than carefully worked out figures'.

Certainly the improvement in the financial position of the FA in the last decade indicates that it is in a position to do more, as we shall see.

The Football Association sits atop all this mass of voluntary effort. Founded in 1863 it is the national governing body for football played by English clubs, whether amateur or professional. Its headquarters are at Lancaster Gate and the association is a rather august body with Her Majesty the Queen as patron and the Duke of Kent as president. All of its ten honorary vice-presidents are Sirs, or Lords or Rt. Hons and most of the officials are in their sixties and seventies. As if conscious of its remoteness, the FA office telephone number is ex-directory. The secretary and the man most often in the limelight as FA spokesman is Denis Follows, Bachelor of Arts and CBE.*

As the national association for England, the Football Association represents the country at meetings of FIFA (International Federation of Football Associations), makes the rules for English football and acts as a court of appeal against decisions by county associations. It is responsible for running the England team, and appointing its manager, Sir Alf Ramsey. It also runs a number of important competitions, notably the FA Cup, the Amateur Cup and the Youth Cup. Apart from these functions, the FA has little to do with the day-to-day running of football, this being undertaken by the county associations and the leagues, of which the Football League is the most important.

The council of the Football Association is the main representative body, totalling eighty-four members, made up of life vice-presidents, representatives from the county associations, representatives from the armed forces and the universities and eight representatives appointed by the Football League.

The Chester Committee's main criticism was of the age of those governing football, a young man's sport, and the fact that three sections of the game were not represented, namely referees, the professional footballers themselves, and club managers and secretaries. They also questioned the need for regional meetings, which assembled together large numbers of people whose travel and subsistence had to be paid for, although they sometimes lasted only fifteen or thirty minutes! They suggested that twice-yearly meetings would be enough.

* Succeeded in June 1973 by Mr. Ted Croker.

As with similar top-heavy organizations, a lot of the work of the FA is handled by committees – around fifteen standing and eight or ten others. Each of the major cup competitions has its own committee, discipline is handled by another, and so on. The Chester Committee took a hard look at the committee system and suggested that the FA lacked a certain 'clarity of purpose' and gave overmuch attention to the affairs of the Football League.

Whilst conceding that an 84-strong council constitutes a useful debating chamber – though one questions just how much knowledge some of the members have of the day-to-day issues of contemporary football – power seems to be concentrated in the hands of a small group of people, comprising the chairman and several other officers. Even the finance and general purposes committee confines itself to the question of finance, and any other matters that are not covered elsewhere in committee.

What is lacking, in the words of the Report, is a more effective central policy and planning committee that could give the FA a sense of direction and would have the experience and breadth of vision to take a general view of the needs of the game.

In spite of its prestige, the financial turnover of the Football Association is not large – about the same as that of an average family-run private company or equivalent to the amount spent on advertising a detergent in any twelve-month period.

Denis Follows reported on the current state of affairs in the April 1972 issue of the *Football Association News*, but this makes difficult reading for the layman. It is difficult also to glean facts. Briefly, it seems that in 1963–4 the Association had a deficit of over £30,000 (the Chester Committee gave a figure of £34,000 and also pointed out that £14,000 of this was accounted for by loss on the sale of an investment). Since then the situation has improved, partly due to the staging of the World Cup in England during the summer of 1966, and partly to the increased contributions from the pools companies and to higher receipts from cup and international matches.

The year 1965 showed a suprlus of £104,000 and this was boosted in the following (World Cup) year to £136,000 – excluding the World Cup receipts. Denis Follows reports that from 1966 to 1969 there has been a surplus of around £135,000 annually – or £153,000 if you add the World Cup profits.

Income is broken down annually into four main sectors:

International matches	162,000
FA Challenge Cup	75,000
Pools companies	75,000
Returns on investments	44,000
Total	£356,000

Additional income is received from radio and television, sale of royalties from various publications, entrance fees and annual subscriptions.

Of this income, a fairly huge slice goes in administrative costs: £95,000 annually according to the *Football Association News*, though the Chester Report gives the 1966 figure as £129,500. Follows's sums look like this:

Administration costs	95,000
Staging non-professional games	32,000
Coaching, instruction	32,000
Taxation	120,000
Total	289,000

The surplus for the year then becomes a staggering £67,000; though the Chester Report gives figures of £104,200 and £136,000 respectively, added to the accumulated surplus fund for the years 1965 and 1966.

At a time when the Association was pleading for more money for coaching and facilities in the amateur game, a further £240,000 was added to its reserves. By the end of 1965, these stood at £320,000 and by 1966 (excluding the World Cup) at £460,000. The World Cup added approximately £200,000 (before tax), and the Chester Report pointed out that if similar surpluses were made annually, by 1970 the accumulated surplus, after allowing for tax, would be over *one million pounds*.

Whilst not exactly pleading poverty, Follows points out in his report that the expenses of the four years (1966–9) show that figures of £266,300 were absorbed for staff salaries, super-annuation, printing, stationery, postage and telegrams; telephone took care of a further £79,900. Against this, only £40,000 a year has been paid to the forty-three county associations (i.e. an average of less than £1,000 each). And in 1970, only £70,000 was spent on coaching.

In addition to appointing regional officers, the Chester Committee recommended that in general the FA should spend more time examining ways in which football both as a sport and an entertainment could be improved and pointed out that football has received very little in the way of grants, either from central or local government. Alongside the development of municipal stadia for professional and important amateur clubs, there should be closer liaison on the question of improving facilities at lower levels.

It is little use, to my mind, printing pictures and stories that appear regularly in the *Football Association News* about poor ground conditions at local level – inadequate changing facilities, lack of baths or showers, muddy and uneven pitches. 'An alert national body ought to have done something about it', says the Report.

Allied to this attitude of chasing one's own tail and getting bogged down in administration, is the need to widen the membership of the Association, by appointing lay experts to specialist committees (public relations, finance, marketing etc.) and by allowing those most closely concerned with the game to have a say. This should include professional or former pro-fessional footballers.

The FA does not have a good record when you come to look at its public relations. Both the start of the 1971–2 and 1972–3 seasons were marked by what the papers called the 'referees revolution' – an attempted crackdown on discipline that led to the booking of 120 players in 8 days, and no fewer than 178 and 8 sent off in the corresponding period at the start of the 1972–3 season.

The clean-up was welcomed by everyone in the game, but what was at fault was the way it was handled: lack of communication between the FA and the professional clubs and players (who attracted the most publicity) caused haphazard interpretation of the new rules and led to further misunderstandings between football's administrators and those who merely play the game for a living.

⌣ Indeed the PFA, the players' union, called a meeting but little if anything came of this and the whole farcical situation repeated itself at the start of the following season. A clear case of the FA being out of touch with the modern professional game.

This lack of professionalism displayed itself later in the year, with the so-called Centenary celebrations held before the Wembley Cup Final. There had been some build-up publicity about whether the hymn singing should continue or not, and eventually a compromise was reached with performer Tommy Steele mounting the rostrum and addressing the crowd in strident tones that did little to add to the dignity of the occasion. This was preceded by a parade of former Cup winners, that degenerated into 'a jumble of flags and bewildered young lads in football strip' (Frank Nicklin, of the *Sun*). The same paper printed extracts from the programme, where the same Centenary message was in some copies written by Denis Follows, in others by Dr Andrew Stephen, the chairman. 'Two minds with but a single idea.'

The most unseemly display, however, arose towards the end of the 1971–2 season, when the niggling disagreements between the Football Association and the League broke into the open and war between the two sides was officially declared. The blame must not attach solely to the FA – the League must bear its fair share.

THE FOOTBALL LEAGUE

In relation to the FA, the League is just one of many football leagues, and it comes under the jurisdiction of the FA simply because it comprises clubs that come from more than three counties, and other leagues like the Northern League or the Southern League are in virtually the same position.

However, to the mass of public and spectators, football means football as played by the ninety-two English League clubs and the attention of the press, television and radio is turned towards their activities, spotlighting star professional players and glamorizing still further the top dozen or more clubs at the head of the First Division.

Because the Football League is the money-making side of the game, its turnover and profits far exceeding those of the FA, it is a powerful influence in the football industry: the clubs and their players are often known nationally and internationally, and it is from among these highly paid professionals that the team to represent England is chosen. Football at this level is a major entertainment industry, and gate receipts and transfer fees run into hundreds of thousands of pounds annually.

League clubs have a heavy programme of games: the season starts early in August and continues until the end of April, with each club playing the other twice. There is also the League Cup, a powerful early-season competition and the FA Cup, both of which culminate in finals at Wembley Stadium. Top clubs are also involved in European soccer, so that the playing season for some clubs has gradually extended, with four to six weeks layoff being the longest some players can expect to enjoy during midsummer.

In addition, international fixtures make heavy demands on top clubs, which have to let players to go join squads representing England, Northern Ireland, Scotland, Wales and Eire, sometime seriously depleting their team strength when they are involved in title or promotion runs or vital cup fixtures. Players suffering injuries in international games are an additional hazard for League clubs.

It is difficult then to imagine that the FA can regard the Football League as just another league and in the case of conflict between the two sides it is likely that the League would win.

The first rumblings of a major row were heard during February and March 1972, and came out into the open after the meeting of League club chairmen at London's Churchill Hotel on 13 April. There had been some discontent about the

D

decision of the FA to charge the BBC a fee of £60,000 for the
television rights in the England v. West Germnay game later
that month. The League felt that a fee of £100,000 was a more
realistic figure and used the opportunity to press for more
control over BBC and ITV fees charged for FA events
(featuring League football players). They also wanted control
of the pool of money resulting from Cup-tie matches and,
another sore point, control of disciplinary procedures, as a result
of anomalies both in referees' booking tactics and resulting
fines and suspensions. The FA had countered with an offer of
some £45,000 more from the Cup pool – less than £500 per
League club – but the League rejected this suggestion as
derisory, bearing in mind the huge FA reserves on which they
were paying Corporation Tax! The League's ultimate weapon
was to threaten to withdraw from the FA Cup and set up a
competition of their own, along the lines of their own
League Cup.

The mutterings continued through most of the summer,
aggravated by side issues like the failure of the England team
under Sir Alf Ramsey and players' complaints that they were
worn out or under too much pressure. It was left to the Minister
for Sport, Eldon Griffiths, to call the two sides together and
following their annual meeting on 2 June, the League announced their new twelve-point plan for handling discipline.

Concessions were made all round, the League winning their
battle to introduce a points-for-fouls system. The players, not
completely sold on the points system, finally won a right of
appeal not only at personal hearings but before an independent
tribunal. And the FA retained overall control of discipline,
with the system of personal hearings continuing, before a
disciplinary committee.

So, just in time for the summer recess, the League and the FA
issued a joint communiqué outlining the new proposals and
peace was declared.

CASH SITUATION

The other interesting factor in the League–FA dispute was

the demand by the League for more cash from the FA to help lower division clubs. We have seen that the League is a much stronger body financially than the FA, and at a time when several transfers topped the £200,000 mark in season 1971–2 it is hard to take their arguments seriously. One solution, and the one proposed by the Chester Committee, would be a football levy board along the lines of the Horserace Levy Board. Another would be the grouping of clubs for Corporation Tax purposes.

The grouping of clubs would allow for a measure of tax relief, under the provisions of the Finance Act of 1967. This means that where companies operate in a group, the profits (and therefore the taxes) of one can be offset against the losses of another. In a small way, large and prosperous clubs, paying high Corporation Tax bills, could adopt smaller not so successful clubs, which were making losses, and what would normally disappear in taxation could be ploughed back into football.

The Chester Committee went so far as to suggest that all the clubs in the League could operate as 'subsidiaries' for taxation purposes, and pointed out that in the period under review, although there was an overall loss of £1·4 million, English League clubs paid £258,000 in Corporation Tax (1965–6). Clearly this is a waste of money, and adopting the grouping principle none of this need have gone to the exchequer, but could have been made available for ground improvements and loans to less successful clubs.

And if, say, Manchester United were to adopt Stockport County, and West Ham adopted Leyton Orient, similar savings could be made, and the smaller clubs, instead of struggling in the shadow of their big brothers, could look to them for support, both moral and financial. As all the clubs except one operate as limited companies there is no reason why ordinary business principles should not be applied to them.

The question of some sort of levy imposed by the government is more interesting. Compared to the spending on the arts, which by any definition is a minority interest, the amount of assistance given to sport is minimal. In 1968–9, the Arts Council spent nearly £3 million on subsidizing opera and ballet alone – the Royal Opera House in London receiving on its own more than £1 million in that year. An Arts Council report recommended that a capital grant of £15 million would be needed to establish a new regional opera centre, backed by annual subsidies of £5 million. The audience for opera and ballet I would estimate as one per cent of the population.

The needs of amateur football alone, played by some one million people weekly, are enormous. At present there are only two major sports centres in England – Lilleshall in Staffordshire and Crystal Palace in London, providing coaching, playing areas and residential accommodation. There is clearly a need for many more such centres, probably non-residential, and improvements are needed on countless pitches, playing areas and dressing-room facilities.

Local authorities are empowered to make grants, largely through their education departments and as a result of the provisions of the Physical Training and Recreation Acts of 1937 and 1958 and the various education and local government acts.

In 1965 the Sports Council was set up, with twenty-four members, originally headed by Mr Denis Howell. Dr Roger Bannister is the current chairman. They are concerned with all sports, and Bannister at the time of writing was urging government grants of up to £3 million annually and talking of the need to spend some £250 million on sport over the next decade. In the second year of its existence, it is interesting to note that some £34,000 only was spent on football, while £87,000 went on cricket!

Some of the needs of the professional game are met by certain levies. The Football League assists member clubs by distributing money received from the pools and by a levy on match receipts, which is distributed equally among the ninety-two clubs. We have already questioned the wisdom of this – why increase the tax burden of the top clubs by such a payment, thus depriving the poorer clubs of a useful handout?

As long ago as the mid-fifties, the pools promoters approached the League with an offer of financial aid. This was turned down until 1959, when an agreement was entered into: this was superseded by another agreement in August 1964, which runs for a period of fifteen years. A royalty of 1 per cent on gross stakes is paid into the League, of which a quarter is paid to the Scottish League. The following January an agreement was also reached with the English Football Association, also for fifteen years, for payment of 0·14 per cent of gross stakes to the FA. This as we have seen brought in £75,000 to the FA in 1971.

The Chester Committee proposed in fact two levies: the first on transfer fees above £25,000 – and it is interesting to note that on the day I was writing this paragraph transfer fees reached another all-time high with the move by fullback David Nish from Leicester to Derby for a record £250,000 fee. The Committee estimated that the levy would produce around £75,000 annually, but in the light of more recent transfer movements this figure could be substantially higher.

The other levy proposed was one of 1 per cent of the gross proceeds of all the pools, and run along the lines of the Horse-race Levy Board. Well over £100 million is staked annually on the pools, and profits are estimated at around £3–4 million. The Horserace Levy Board collects money from both book-makers and the tote, and raises some £3 million annually by these means which are ploughed back into projects like horse-breeding and veterinary science. The suggested levy on football pools would, it is estimated, bring in a further £1 million in addition to the £1 million already paid by the pools promotors.

This is still a fractional amount compared to the grants paid out in support of the arts in Great Britain: £17 million in 1969–70.

THE FOOTBALL LEAGUE AND THE CLUBS

The League suffers from the same sense of remoteness as the FA and this time the reasons are purely geographical: their headquarters are situated in, of all places, Lytham St Anne's on the north-west Lancashire coast. Secretary Alan Hardaker has his house next door. It is this remoteness that is a bane to club secretaries, who have to make dramatic dashes to the League HQ to register the transfers of players in time for the Saturday game.

The line-up of the League's personnel is a more mundane affair than the FA's: president is Len Shipman of Leicester, and there are two vice-presidents, Mr. S. Bolton of Leeds and Burnley pieman Bob Lord. There is an eight-man management committee made up of directors of football clubs.

The League sponsors its own main competition, the League Cup, known for years as 'Hardaker's baby'. Introduced only in 1960, with a lukewarm majority of just fifteen, pessimists predicted that within three years it would collapse. In the first year five League clubs refused to participate, in the second year ten – including seven of the top ten clubs. The result was that the 1962 final between a Second and a Fourth Division side only pulled in some 30,000 spectators.

The turning point came in 1966: the old home-and-away final was scrapped in favour of a Saturday afternoon final at Wembley; and the UEFA Cup committee agreed to accept the winners of the Cup for the European tournament. The revitalized final attracted a 98,000 crowd and was watched by millions on television. Some clubs still remained aloof, notably Manchester United, and it was not until the League's annual general meeting in 1971 that a resolution was passed making it compulsory for all clubs to enter. In the 1973 final, Spurs beat Norwich by one goal to nil, before a crowd of 100,000. Gate receipts also reached an all time high.

The main criticism in the early days of the League Cup was that the fixture list was already too crowded, and yet curiously enough the competition gained in popularity just at the time when more and more clubs were starting to participate in European football and other competitions like the Watney and Texaco Cups and the Anglo-Italian Tournament were gaining interest. The 1966 World Cup revived interest in football generally, leading to more television coverage. The League Cup also has the advantage of being played fairly early in the season, culminating in the important rounds being staged between October and March.

The increase in attendance and gate receipts meant that the clubs benefited from the share-out: in 1963-4 each participating club received a mere £327; in 1972 this sum had risen to just over £2,000. And aggregate attendances have grown from just over a million in 1960–1 to nearly 2½ million in 1971–2.

Fixture congestion is still a problem, particularly for the top clubs and early in 1972 Alan Hardaker summed up the situation thus:

'Look at the fixture list for the eight weeks after 1 April: we have the Easter games, two European Cup rounds, the FA Cup Semi-Finals, the UEFA Cup Final, the FA Cup Final, the Home International Championships, the European Cup Final, the European Cup Winners' Cup Final, not to mention all the normal League games (until the end of April), and any fixtures postponed from earlier in the year.'

At that stage, it was conceivable that Arsenal might have been aiming at the FA Cup, the League Cup, and the European Cup. At the same time, England team manager Sir Alf Ramsey was asking for the release of five of their first-team squad for international duty and others were required for the Scottish, Welsh and Irish national squads.

Hardaker's outburst came as the result of the FA's demand for the England squad to be released by the League clubs for a fortnight in preparation for the important European Championship game against West Germany on 29 April. England lost by three goals to one and then drew 0–0 in the second leg in Berlin, and the poor performance of the national side led to press calls for the resignation of Ramsey and a complete rethink about English international football.

The conflict between club and country has always been a thorny one, but came to a head with the suspension later in the year of Chelsea's Alan Hudson and Derby's Colin Todd who failed to respond to Ramsey's call, pleading exhaustion or domestic problems as the excuse. We will look at this situation more closely in the section on the England team, and also on players in trouble.

TELEVISED FOOTBALL

Football makes quite a lot of money out of televised games, but because the club whose match is screened can receive as little as £60 'disturbance allowance' for the privilege, some managers, among them Brian Clough, have at one time or another actually banned cameras from their grounds, in order to deny other clubs a chance to scrutinize their tactics. The games that are to be televised are not announced until late on Saturday afternoon, in an attempt to avoid a fall-off in ground spectators, but the arrival of the television vans in a back street behind the club the day before the game often lets the cat out of the bag.

Despite arguments that television has a bad effect on attendances, I have seen no convincing evidence in support of this theory. On the contrary, it is often the televised games that attract record gates, proving that football enthusiasts can be drawn to an attractive fixture whether it is going to be screened later or not. Invariably these well-attended fixtures have included those in small provincial towns (e.g. Ipswich, Leicester) where the arrival of the television vans at the ground on the day before the game was virtually impossible to conceal.

Under their contract with the Football League, only forty-five minutes of action can be shown – just half the game – and the resulting presentation owes a lot to the skill of the sports editor. There are conflicting arguments whether television has killed wrestling in the public halls, or alternatively put what was formerly a minority sport firmly on the map. Certainly television has aroused interest in sports like motorcycle speedway and rally cross and to deny television the opportunity to show football is to take a backward step at a time when everything should be geared towards attracting a fringe audience to the game.

Football gets around £350,000 annually from the BBC and the independent companies, and this is shared among the clubs (all ninety-two in the League), a disturbance allowance for the clubs whose matches are televised, the players' union, the League and the FA. For a long time the BBC has argued in favour of more coverage and in 1967 put up a proposal to pay £3 million over a three-year period for the right to transmit a live match every Thursday evening – a curious choice as hardly any matches are played on Thursdays, the clubs' traditional day off.

The Joint Television Committee of the League and FA rejected the idea, fearing that matches chosen for their high entertainment value would affect Saturday afternoon gates. This could well be true. According to figures published by National Opinion Polls in 1967, 38 per cent of those who claimed they were interested in football said they did not go to matches because they could watch on television. And 44 per cent of the population aged 16 and over watched football on television at least once a week.

Clearly matches have to be chosen from among the top teams, otherwise viewers will simply switch off. The BBC contract states that they must take ten Second Division matches and four from the Third or Fourth each season and in laying down these conditions the football authorities are merely digging their own grave that much deeper. Choice of matches is even further restricted when up to half a dozen First Division grounds are not well enough lit for colour television.

Perhaps the idea is to present a balanced view of football and occasionally one can witness exciting games taking place in the Second and lower divisions, just as a match between two top clubs can inexplicably fail to rise to expectations. But as another mass of viewers is already claiming there is too much sport on television, it is logical that what is shown should be the best. After Wimbledon fortnight or the Munich Olympics, who wants to watch highlights from Grimsby Town against Tranmere Rovers?

It is clearly foolish to deny football a powerful medium of wider publicity. It is up to those who run the industry to make football compete favourably with other attractions and not attempt to deny a mass audience – up to ten millions for an average sports programme – the opportunity to watch top-clase football in the comfort of their own homes. One more match a week is not going to make all that much difference and the additional income could go some way towards solving the financial problems of clubs in the Third and Fourth Divisions.

Chapter 4

The Players' Union

In the same way that the employers formed themselves into associations in the shape of the FA and the Football League, way back in 1907 the players (and trainers) formed their own union, registering as a trade union in December of the following year. Subscriptions are still ridiculously low – compared to similar professional associations outside football.

Permanent secretary of the union, or Professional Footballers' Association as it is now called, is a kindly 55-year-old ex-footballer, Cliff Lloyd, who occupies offices inside Manchester's Corn Exchange building. He is assisted by a committee of eight players, and the present chairman is Derek Dougan, an Irishman who plays for Wolves. He is the seventh man to have served with Lloyd – others have included Noel Cantwell and Terry Neill, and, possibly most famous of all, Jimmy Hill.

The committee serves for two years, half the members coming up for re-election each year. They represent football's elder statesmen, Bobby Charlton and Terry Venables among them.

First signs of trouble came early on in the union's history, when the FA withdrew recognition of the union only two years after its formation and only after a partial strike by players was the dispute settled. Footballers' pay was the burning question almost from the outset, and the union's history is peppered with attempts to raise the maximum wage for professional players: it was £4 a week in 1901 and rose to £9 after the First World War. It was actually *reduced* within three years, when the

League Management Committee voted to cut the maximum wage to £8 in 1921, after the union had asked for £10.

So it remained until 1947 when a new *minimum* wage was established: £7 per week during the season, reducing to £5 during the summer. A skilled craftsman would have earned £3 to £4 a week at that time.

In 1953 Cliff Lloyd became secretary of the union. Born in Helsby, Cheshire, where he still lives, he worked in a factory in Liverpool, and signed for Liverpool FC in 1937, playing alongside Matt Busby. He spent most of the war years as a PTI and then came to London and played for Fulham. Afterwards he moved to Bristol Rovers, but a broken leg at the age of 27 forced him to retire from the game. He returned north and opened up the union's office in Manchester.

The next seven years were a continuing battle for higher wages for footballers and the abolition of the ceiling on wages. Lloyd found a useful ally in his old team mate Matt Busby, who in 1957 wrote a newspaper article proposing the abolition of the maximum wage. Rumours of under-the-counter payments to players, notably Sunderland where two players were suspended by the FA made a mockery of the present wage system, Busby pointed out. The maximum was raised that year to £17 a week, and a year later rose to £20, with League secretary Alan Hardaker insisting that if players played better they would get more money!

Meanwhile, a lanky, bearded player from Fulham had been elected chairman of the Players' Union in the uncompromising shape of Jimmy Hill. He and Lloyd continued to press two demands: abolition of the maximum wage and a completely new contract system for players, getting rid once and for all of the retain and transfer rights of the clubs. In 1960 they had talks with the League and when these were abruptly broken off by Hardaker, Hill promptly reported a state of 'industrial dispute' to the Ministry of Labour.

The Ministry appointed a conciliation officer and in desperation the League met the following November to consider ways of pacifying the players: but suggestions of wage increases, bonus payments and incentives, and appearance money put forward by various clubs were thrown out and the meeting ended in confusion.

Meanwhile Jimmy Hill and Cliff Lloyd organized regional meetings of players in London, Birmingham and Manchester and were given the go-ahead by their members to take whatever action they thought was necessary. Press and public alike were amazed at the players' strength and solidarity, yet in spite of this the League still rejected the players' proposals at a meeting on 9 December.

Further regional meetings of players were then held and just before Christmas they gave formal notice that if their demands were not met all professional footballers would come out on strike on the following 21 January (1961).

The football clubs, still unable to grasp the full impact of the situation, announced that they would continue the programme of fixtures using amateur players, though it was far from clear whether these footballers would have turned out as 'blacklegs' in opposition to their professional colleagues.

The Ministry of Labour intervened again and drew up a plan which seemed acceptable to both sides. The clubs met on 9 January, and offered to abolish the maximum wage but would make no concessions on the retain and transfer clauses in players' contracts. After further meetings, the players rejected this: the retain and transfer system was open to abuse, as a player could be tied to his club indefinitely, receiving only the minimum wage, until the club felt good and ready to transfer him.

It was only on 18 January – three days before the start of the proposed strike, that the then Minister of Labour Mr John Hare personally intervened and agreement was reached: the maximum wage was abolished and players' contract improved.

But by the following March the clubs had met again and promptly rescinded their agreement about contracts, and it was only after the result of the George Eastham case two years later that the present contract system was adopted.

Eastham, a player with Newcastle United, brought a test case against his club and refused to re-sign for them when they rejected his request for a transfer. He was backed by the PFA and eventually in July 1963 Mr Justice Wilberforce in the High Court declared that the rules of the FA and League relating to the retention and transfer for professional footballers were 'in unreasonable restraint of trade'. Eastham won his case and moved to Arsenal for a £47,000 fee.

In the following May, the League were forced to amend their rules and gave players the right of appeal against the terms offered them by a club at the end of their contracts. Soon after, a permanent arbitration tribunal was set up to look into disputes.

In 1967, the union won another important concession for players transferred by their clubs: there would be a levy of 10 per cent, of which 5 per cent went to the players and 5 per cent to the players' provident fund. The provident fund had been set up in 1949 by the League, and receives money from transfer fees as mentioned, and also the League pays 10 per cent on the annual earnings of players earning less than £2,000 a year. A player can, at 35, if he has ceased to be a League player, collect the benefits that have accumulated in his name.

The players' accident insurance scheme is designed to help the clubs rather than the individual (injured) player. The club receives a substantial capital payment, depending on the value attached to the player, while the player receives a basic payment while injured, and £1,000 or less if he has to give up the game.

The Chester Committee were sharply critical of these arrangements and proposed a modern type of contributory pension scheme for players, with lump-sum payments on their retirement from football (to help them transfer to another occupation) and a deferred pension at 60 or 65. They also recommended that a collective insurance scheme should be set up to cover injuries to players.

Most of these recommendations were put to the League in 1970 by the PFA, who proposed a tax on transfer fees to pay the premiums for a pension scheme. They also pressed for a minimum wage for all professionals – a modest enough £1,080 per year – and an ending of the option clause in players' contracts which still favours the clubs. The proposals were rejected and chairman Derek Dougan was heard to remark, blandly, 'that Rome was not built in a day'.

Clearly, in spite of the high earnings of most First Division players, pay and conditions in football are not good and there are many things that are wrong with the present system of contracts, options and transfers. Big money transfers and the life styles of a few top players tend to give the impression that everything in the garden is rosy.

FAILURE OF THE UNION

The players' union fails to be a completely effective voice in football for a number of reasons.

Its paid staff is ridiculously small: for a long time it consisted of Cliff Lloyd and a secretary. Lloyd himself is a tireless worker, but is forced to spend a large amount of his time travelling to represent players at disciplinary hearings. This means he spends a lot of time out of the office and the wear and tear on him must be considerable, depriving him of the opportunity to concentrate on wider issues.

There is also a distinct apathy among players generally about the affairs of the union. Collecting the monthly subscriptions takes up valuable secretarial time in correspondence and reminders, and delegates at club level find they have to buttonhole their colleagues in the dressing-room on pay day to collect the outstanding dues. Clearly subs are too low, as players are well paid by ordinary job standards. (Subscriptions to the National Union of Journalists for instance are nearly twice this amount.)

The PFA is perennially short of money, and this situation could be improved by raising the subscriptions well above their present level. Nor should it be impossible either to deduct payments directly from players' salaries as in other unions, or persuade players to send an annual cheque in payment if they find the other alternative irksome. Prompt receipt of dues in this way would relieve the already overworked office staff and leave them time to devote to other matters.

There is also surprisingly little interest in union affairs among top players, the ones that are household names in the game. This may result from shyness or simple apathy, and it is a subject I have broached with a number of prominent First Division players, who, to my mind, should be vigorous spokesmen for football. Instead they are invariably wrapped up in their own playing careers, early marriage and growing business interests outside the game and it is shameful to find that only players like the present chairman Derek Dougan or his predecessor Terry Neill – both incidentally Irishmen – are articulate spokesmen on the wider issues of football.

It is only when a player is in trouble – over a clause in his contract, a suspension or pay problems – that he turns to the union and a large part of Cliff Lloyd's day is spent answering letters and telephone calls about players' personal problems.

Lloyd himself is painfully aware of the needs of players to do something to prepare themselves for another career when they leave football. All too often this is something that is neglected. Club managers appear to do little to help, and there are numerous demands on a player's time in terms of training, mid-week games and travel to away fixtures that make it difficult to persevere with a course of study.

The union have recently appointed an education officer to help players learn about career opportunities outside football and run courses on business management. But the results are disappointing. Few players know about or take advantage of grants and facilities available for further study, and it is usually in the lower divisions – among the players earning £35 a week – that footballers take the trouble to prepare for their futures.

Many I spoke to were confident that when the time came 'something would turn up'; others are convinced that a career outside football will ruin their game. Some clubs encourage outside interests (e.g. Manchester City), others discourage them. It is clearly an area where the union has a lot of work to do.

Already they maintain a sort of unemployment register and

try and help find jobs for players at the end of their playing careers, or even during the close season. A lot of players obviously know how to help themselves and put money into sports shops or ladies' hairdressers.

Relations with employers, the League, are as good as most other trade unions with their bosses, though Dougan declared himself dissatisfied with the results of a meeting with the League and the FA, the managers and secretaries and the referees, to discuss the so-called 'referees revolution' at the start of the 1971–2 season. A year later, when the situation repeated itself at the start of the new season, it was as if nothing had been discussed.

Clearly the union must do more to make itself felt. With increased funds a newsletter could be published, keeping players informed of meetings (notoriously badly attended) and current developments, as well as acting as a platform for the PFA viewpoint. Their situation in Manchester, while setting them down in the midst of one of soccer's acknowledged strongholds, does make them rather remote from the Midland and London clubs, to say nothing of players on the south coast as far away as Brighton, Portsmouth and Southampton.

Lloyd will obviously one day need a successor, yet no one seems in line for the job. He also needs assistance in the shape of people able to attend hearings and relieve him of the many day-to-day administrative distractions.

Clearly the players must organize themselves better and the lead should be given by articulate First Division stars (a job for football's nucleus of graduates?) used to talking to the press and appearing on radio and television. It is up to those who have taken most out of the game to put something back into it for the sake of the general good.

Players' problems can cover a wide range. They include serious or long-term injuries; contract problems; transfer situations that do not work out; problems of adjustment to the end of a playing career; problems of being in the limelight; being dropped from the first team and unhappy in the reserves; domestic difficulties, and conflicts with football management. We will look at a few typical examples of each situation.

INJURIES TO PLAYERS

Injuries can wreck or seriously disrupt the career of a promising and successful player. Most serious are leg injuries – a broken leg kept Chelsea's young Ian Hutchinson out of football for over a season after he came to prominence in the Chelsea–Leeds Cup Final at the end of the 1969–70 season. He started light training at the beginning of the 1972–3 season, following treatment at a rehabilitation centre, only to return to the first team and suffer another injury. In March 1973, Hutchinson was back at an RAF unit trying to get fit again.

Tony Green, now with Newcastle United, spent almost a whole season out of the game with his former club, Blackpool. Fortunately this tough little Scotsman recovered sufficiently to warrant a £90,000 transfer fee when he moved to Newcastle United in the early months of the 1971–2 season.

Often an injury occurs soon after a promising transfer move: this happened to former Crystal Palace and Luton player Roger Hoy, when he moved to Cardiff. He played a few games for them and then spent the rest of the season out of the team through injury.

Spurs man Roger Morgan got kicked on the knee during a League game in 1970, which led to a cartilage operation and several months lay-off. Eddie Gray of Leeds dislocated his shoulder during a Fairs Cup match in Turin, had an operation only two weeks before the start of a new season and spent six weeks with his arm strapped across his chest, but he kept himself cheerful, going to the Leeds ground every day to watch the other players training.

Arsenal goalkeeper Bob Wilson won a lot of sympathy when he fell awkwardly during Arsenal's FA Cup semi-final in 1971: the result was a cartilage injury and many months of frustrating solo exercises during the summer months to get fit for the new season. Another goalkeeper, Gordon Banks of Stoke City, suffered a serious eye injury in November 1972 as the result of a car accident and there were doubts that he would ever play football again.

A player's fitness, or lack of it, can occasionally jeopardize a

E

promising transfer move, and perhaps the most famous case is that of West Bromwich Albion's Asa Hartford. In November 1971 Hartford 'moved' to Leeds United for £170,000, then three days later Leeds announced that the deal was off and Hartford was told he had a heart condition. The player was welcomed back to scenes of unprecedented emotion by his old club, who promised 'to stick by him'. Two days later, a further medical examination revealed a not too serious hole-in-the-heart condition and the player was given the all clear to continue football. While not denying Leeds's right to have their players one hundred per cent fit, it is the handling of the affair that is open to question: the club were issuing statements about a 'medical condition' and leaving Hartford, and the public and football press, to guess the worst. In the event, the situation proved far less serious than anticipated, and a young man could have been spared the shock of being half-informed about his condition on the morning of what would have been his first game for his new club.

TRANSFER PROBLEMS

Sometimes transfers do not work out for other reasons, or in fact never happen at all. The season 1971–2 showed a marked increase in the use of players on loan – Fulham tried the tactic with Alan Mullery, who eventually signed for the club. A more distressing case was that of a young Luton forward Viv Busby. A shy local boy from High Wycombe, Busby was loaned to First Division Newcastle United in anticipation of a transfer. He found himself plunged into a class of football that was way above him and involved in a struggle for First Division survival. Still he did not disgrace himself and in spite of a bout of influenza he played in four League games, an FA Cup tie and a reserve game – scoring four goals.

Newcastle had already spent heavily in the transfer market – including the purchase of Busby's former team mate and close friend Malcolm MacDonald from Luton, for £150,000. They were relying on a good run in the FA Cup to bring more money into the kitty. Drawn in the third round against tiny Hereford, they finally lost to this then non-League club in the replay. The following Monday the Newcastle manager Joe Harvey called Busby into the office and informed him that the deal was off: there was simply no money to pay for him.

Busby returned to his old club a disillusioned young man and it was left to Alec Stock, the then Luton manager, to decry the situation: 'What have they done to my boy' he asked, adding that Busby was returned to him 'in a state of shock and hurt'.

Busby's was not the only loan scandal of the season: Manchester City loaned a spare goalkeeper to Coventry, and Crystal Palace their centre-half Bobby Bell to Norwich – who promptly beat Millwall the following Saturday and clinched their own promotion to the First Division. But the case of Alan Mullery is even more strange, as evidence of how a world-class player can experience the ups and downs of a career all within the space of a few days.

Alan Mullery, thirty years old, fifteen years in football and with thirty-six international caps to his credit, was loaned by Tottenham to his old club Fulham half-way through the 1971-2 season. He had been out of football for several weeks with a pelvic injury and jumped at the chance of regaining League experience with his former club. The move was not popular and Mullery was booed at away games. He was then abruptly recalled by Tottenham, whose own team was depleted by injuries, for a European match against Milan. He played well and scored a goal. Even more surprising was his recall to the England squad to play against Germany. He did not appear and shortly afterwards announced his resignation from international football. Fulham then stepped in and bought Mullery at the start of the new season for a fee of £60,000, and the former England man found himself back in the Second Division.

Mullery's problems are not unique, of course. Every player must reach the end of his career one day, but the slide down into the reserves, then a transfer to a Second or Third Division club is not graceful. Many players who featured in the England team at the time of the World Cup (1966) have disappeared out of football. Dave Mackay had a short run at Derby before going to Swindon as team manager. Geoff Hurst has left West Ham and gone to Stoke. Jimmy Greaves is looking after his business. Ian St John retired to South African football. England fullback Keith Newton, after a near disastrous season with Everton, moved to Second Division Burnley on a free transfer. Finally the great Bobby Charlton was left out of the Manchester United team in favour of a younger man and moved into management at Preston.

Not all players go out with a bang – a lucrative benefit game, followed by a coaching or managerial job. Nothing is more depressing than the annual posting of names at the end of each season, players the club has decided they do not need any more. They include younger men whose luck or talents have not quite measured up. Manchester United released six players on free transfers in 1971, including Scottish international Ian Ure.

TRYING TO GET AWAY

Another facet of the transfer situation is the case of the player trying desperately to get away from his club: his reasons can vary from a chance to better himself, the urge to earn more money or the fact that he cannot hold his place in the first team. A player who has been in this situation is Eamonn Dunphy of Millwall. Dunphy is an Irish international who started his football life as an apprentice with Manchester United at the same time as George Best. He then moved to York for a small fee, and then to Millwall. His delicate type of ball-playing football, it might be argued, does not suit the aggressive style of the dockland club and for five years to my knowledge Dunphy has been trying to get away.

At the end of one contract – a year plus a year's option – he refused to re-sign and appealed to the Football League. All the while, he was retained on his old contract and basic salary, with the effect that he was losing money every week. In the end he had to re-sign. The same situation occurred a couple of seasons later, with Dunphy in and out of the first team, but Millwall still refusing to let go. In the end, he collected his cards and walked out – the only solution for a player in this situation.

A player in a similar situation was Arsenal's Peter Marinello. Marinello, a frail young Scottish winger, was bought by Arsenal from Hibernian for, at that time, an exceptional fee of £100,000. He made an impressive debut and scored a goal against Manchester United. He was subsequently dropped from the first team and spent two whole seasons out of it. Unfortunately, his arrival at Highbury was a much publicized affair: with his flowing hair and trendy clothes, the 20-year-old was hailed as another George Best.

Clearly the situation was not satisfactory for a young player and the press reported several times that he requested either a permanent first team place – or a move to another club. Arsenal however appeared to want to hang grimly on. Their argument was that Marinello had to get used to the demands of English football, that he was bought as an investment for the future. Clearly this was nonsense. Marinello was purchased for his individuality and a natural body-swerve. He was continually brainwashed. Then in December 1972 Arsenal finally agreed to Marinello's request for a move and he was put on the list for a reported £100,000. He eventually moved to Second Division Portsmouth – not one of soccer's glamour clubs – the following May for £80,000. What is inexcusable is that his former club held onto him for so long.

Another player transferred in a blaze of publicity was a baby-faced lad from Wolverhampton, Alun Evans. Bill Shankly bought him for Liverpool for £100,000. 'Alun has the heart of a lion, guts, enthusiasm and my faith in him has been completely justified', he said at the time. Within a season, Evans was dropped. 'If he was up for sale again for £100,000 I'd buy him tomorrow', Shankly had said. What went wrong?

Two seasons later and a stone or two heavier, Evans moved to newly promoted Aston Villa in the Second Division.

Consider also the case of Bobby Ferguson, the West Ham goalkeeper. He was in dispute with his club at the start of the 1972-3 season and when the problem could not be resolved was promptly dropped from the first team into the reserves. 'While he has contract problems the player cannot concentrate on his game', declared the club. Curiously he was good enough for them before the dispute arose, and forcing a player into the reserve team in this high-handed manner can only be described as a coercive tactic of the most sinister kind. Two months later and still out of the first team, Ferguson was reported to be 'not available' when the idea of his replacing Gordon Banks (out of football with an eye injury) at Stoke City was suggested.

Clearly in spite of elaborate scouting systems and all the possible checks on a player's performance mistakes can be made. And players may struggle with one club and unaccountably blossom with another. Many rejects somehow make it. Scunthorpe parted with Liverpool star Kevin Keegan for only £35,000. They let their goalkeeper Ray Clemence go for even less (£20,000). Tranmere Rovers sold Roy McFarland to Derby for £35,000 only. Colin Bell went to Manchester City from Bury for a mere £45,000. Mike Summerbee joined him from Swindon for less. Steve Perryman of Spurs was turned down by his local club Brentford. Alan Ball was turned down by Wolves, Tony Currie by Queens Park Rangers.

Of course, a lot of players at some time or another are dissatisfied with their clubs. If it is a collective feeling, it is usually over pay. This, for example, led to a strike threat by Falkirk players early in the 1972–3 season, which was only resolved two hours before the Saturday afternoon game. Nine Spurs players led a revolt at White Hart Lane for more cash at the start of the same season, the result of a dispute that had been simmering throughout the close season, following the club's success in European football. And Arsenal's home-grown star Charlie George put in a transfer request, together with Eddie Kelly and John Roberts – together worth around £500,000 on the market. They were protesting that under the Arsenal system of paying bonuses for long service to the club the younger players were not getting a fair deal. Two other players, Ray Kennedy and Sammy Nelson, had also been in dispute over pay. The club pompously replied in the case of the other three by granting their requests for a move – surely a bad case of personnel relations.

Domestic problems can also mar a player's career. Chelsea's Alan Hudson went through a difficult time during his early career at Stamford Bridge when he walked out of the family home, following a row with his father. A couple of seasons later he pleaded domestic problems as excuse for not taking part in an England Under-23 tour, along with Derby's Colin Todd. Whatever reasons the two players gave to an inquisitive press the situation highlighted a question that had been aired for most of the second half of the season 1971–2 – the problems of fatigue and strain on top-class players.

STRAIN AT THE TOP

Francis Lee was one of the players to crack up: he had a breakdown and later confessed that he had been working up to eighteen hours a day, either playing football, training, attending local functions or working at his paper factory in Manchester. Other players were meanwhile complaining about the length of the playing season and proposed tours abroad during the summer months. A tour by the England team to Turkey and Yugoslavia was subsequently called off, after protests by the players.

Players declared they were near breaking point, racked with injuries and in need of a rest. 'The game', declared Alan Ball, 'is killing us'. The decision provoked mixed reactions in the press. Veteran manager Joe Mercer decided it was a good thing, while Scotland team manager Tommy Docherty talked about 'pampered players'. In the *Daily Mail*, 37-year-old Jackie Charlton declared 'These kids shock me', referring to the Hudson/Todd affair.

Are the pressures too great? The same paper analysed a week in the life of Alan Ball: flying home to Manchester from Berlin to see his sick father (Sunday); driving to Sheffield to appeal against an FA caution (Tuesday); back to London for a day with his family (Wednesday); training with the England team (Thursday); train and coach trip to Cardiff (Friday); take part in Wales *v*. England game (Saturday). Ball felt he was entitled to six weeks off in twelve months' activity.

Ian Wooldridge of the *Mail* however disagreed, under a banner headline 'There are no trade union hours in the big league'. He had little sympathy for professional footballers, and cited the case of golfer Lee Trevino who in the previous twenty days had travelled 11,000 miles to win the American, Canadian and British Open Championships. Or Miss Evonne Goolagong who allowed herself one day off in the seven-week preparation period for Wimbledon.

The Todd/Hudson affair has more serious consequences, particularly as the pair of promising youngsters were punished with a two-year international ban by the FA – clearly a case of cutting off your nose to spite your face. The action by the players reflects little more than a sign of the times – simply too much football; and in the case of Hudson, bad judgement by England team manager Sir Alf Ramsey. Hudson was called up for the home internationals series and then not played, missing his club's tour of the West Indies as a result of standing by for duty. It is simple to imagine the player's reaction when called again for duty with the England Under-23 squad. As Brian Glanville put it in *The Sunday Times*, a case of 'snubbing the snubber'.

THE MAN WHO ROCKED A CLUB

No examination of players' problems would be complete without a look at the saga of George Best. His is an interesting case – a mixture of outstanding football talent coupled with a pop star ambience – that culminated in his early retirement from football and the sacking of his club's manager, assistant and trainer.

Best joined Manchester United as a sixteen-year-old apprentice from his native Belfast and within a couple of years was displaying his precocious talent on the football field. Added to his displays of skill and power to score goals, he was the first player to wear his hair long and promote the fashionable boutique-owning image of the modern player. He gradually gathered round him a group of 'business advisers', an agent, and secured lucrative contracts to model clothes or endorse products.

All was not right, however. Best was reportedly sick of the glare of publicity and the newspapers started to carry stories of his late nights and wild life, interspersed with dashes to London to live it up in the King's Road or Jermyn Street. Then a few days before his twenty-sixth birthday in May 1972 Best announced that he was retiring from football 'for good'. In a heart-searching article in the *Sunday Mirror* he declared himself a mental and physical wreck and talked of visits to doctors and psychiatrists and of his late nights and drinking. He had fled to a Spanish holiday resort and there he stayed, ignoring pleas from Sir Matt Busby, his team mates and his own Northern Ireland international squad.

Best's retirement was, however, short-lived. Once the close season was over he returned home to Manchester and after a half-hearted wigging from his club and an injunction to move in with team mate Paddy Crerand, he started to get ready for the new season. Somehow a little of the Best magic had worn off. Who could now believe anything he said after such an about face? Coupled with his own problems, Best found his team struggling and soon there was talk of United heading for relegation after a string of disastrous games.

Best himself had a couple of lapses from training but, presumably because Manchester United had more than enough troubles as it was, he got away with fines and suspensions by the club. Then at the beginning of December, he did his biggest disappearing act ever, flying to London and dancing at Tramps discotheque while his team struggled. Again he returned and after a search lasting two or three days, a meeting was hastily arranged between Best, Sir Matt Busby and the club chairman Louis Edwards. His suspension was apparently lifted and his name taken off the transfer list.

While the football world gasped in astonishment at this treatment of their wayward player and the apparent slighting of manager Frank O'Farrell, United went down 5–0 in a disastrous game at Crystal Palace. There was speculation that O'Farrell would be forced to resign and everyone eagerly awaited a meeting of the United board to be held the following Tuesday.

The outcome of this meeting staggered even the most seasoned football reporter: O'Farrell got the sack, and along with him his assistant Malcolm Musgrove and trainer John Aston. The board also decreed that Best would never play for the club again.

In a way, Best had the last laugh. Unknown to the board he delivered by hand a personal letter announcing his complete resignation from football – thereby effectively depriving the club of the quarter of a million pounds or more they might have gained by selling him on the transfer market!

A lot has been written in the press about George Best and the United affair and sports writers were not slow to attack the wayward Irishman. Certainly he needed firm guidance and his story illustrates the lack of genuine counsel and friendship that a player in his unique position has to suffer. This was poignantly emphasized by the type of offer that was made while he was on the transfer list: to go to Bournemouth and supplement his income by being shown off in a night club owned by the chairman. Or to become a disc jockey under the guidance of Jimmy Savile.

Whether these offers were genuine or not, clearly their authors misunderstood the character of George Best. As one player put it who had trained with him as an apprentice at United ten years earlier: 'George hasn't changed, only his hair has got longer'.

The lessons to be drawn from the Best case, and indeed from all the examples of players who find themselves in one sort of trouble or another, is the lack of guidance and genuine help available to them in times of crisis.

Most footballers come from very ordinary backgrounds, yet exceptional ability can quickly put them in the surtax bracket. If they move from club to club, they have to leave home and unless they are married they have to live in lodgings approved by the club. They are bound to have personal problems, yet rarely is there anyone to whom they can turn for guidance. Managers and club staff generally do not possess the personal qualities needed to counsel youngsters and in any event are bogged down with their own problems of survival and producing a winning side.

It is in the early days that youngsters have a lot of time on their hands. After the morning training session, there is not much left in small provincial towns except the betting shop or the bowling alley. Comparatively few young players develop outside interests and in some cases these seem to be positively discouraged by the club. So footballers marry young and marriage is regarded as the cure-all for Best's and every other player's problems.

There is a need for someone with the necessary qualifications, a psychologist even, to be available to advise players – about their contracts, their future prospects, their transfers, their outside interests. A move to another club is not just a financial transaction: the player should be encouraged to examine whether he will be *happy* in his new surroundings and whether the transfer will help his long-term career prospects.

It is unfortunate that a lead does not come from the players' union. Football may be a team game, but, especially at the top, it is made up of two thousand very lonely individuals.

Chapter 5

Slaves United: a look at Players' Contracts, Wages and the Transfer Business

RECRUITMENT

It is not commonly known that from the age of 13 years onwards, a promising youngster can be effectively tied to the club that takes an interest in him from that tender age until the end of his playing career, by a series of one-way options (on the club's side) that in any other profession would almost certainly be regarded as unreasonable restraint of freedom.

There are usually three stages in the career of the professional footballer: associate schoolboy, apprentice professional and full professional. Of course not all professional players come into the game in this way, which is in itself a condemnation of the apprenticeship system, as we shall see in due course.

Even at schoolboy and junior level, competitive football is closely bound up in regulations administered by the English Schools Football Association. This august body, founded in 1863, is run rather like a mini FA and claims affiliated membership of over 12,000 schools. Similar associations in Scotland and Wales boast 1,260 and 430 members respectively. So you can see that football, apart from the activity of the well-known League clubs, is an activity involving thousands of young players in conditions ranging from waste ground with a set of improvised goalposts to schoolboy internationals that attract 100,000 gates at Wembley. There are in fact over 33,000 recognized amateur football clubs, all playing in some kind of local, district or county league, up and down the country.

Over a number of years it became noticeable that the efficient system of selective trials and representative games run by the ESFA was becoming a hunting ground for scouts from the professional clubs and there are stories that at some school-boy games as many as half-a-dozen masters were assigned to the task of keeping club representatives away from the young players. We are talking of boys of twelve or thirteen being offered financial inducements to sign for League clubs, in direct contravention of the rules of the Football League.

The situation got so bad that in 1965 the League was forced to draw up a set of regulations, now contained in their famous Rule 48, that created a class of players known as associated schoolboys and attempting in some ways to regularize the then position.

The rules are comprehensive, but briefly, they allow clubs to sign youngsters over the age of thirteen 'for the purposes of training and coaching', provided that priority is always given to school activities. Boys under fifteen cannot actually play for the club, and over fifteen they require the headmaster's consent. They cannot sign for more than one club, and no club can have more than forty associated schoolboys on their books – broken down into age groups, that is fifteen boys in the age group 13–14 and so on, up to a maximum of ten over school-leaving age.

Clubs are not supposed to put pressure on their schoolboys to sign apprentice forms, and no registration of a young apprentice will be accepted by the Football League without the written consent of the boy's headmaster or the local educa-tion authority. As a result of the scheme, some 1,200 schoolboys are registered with the League as attached to various clubs – the largest group (around 500) being in the 15–16 age group.

The League in its wisdom hoped that the new regulations would end at least some of the abuses relating to young players. This is unfortunately not the case. Parents themselves are often to blame – shopping around trying to sell their son to the highest under-the-table bidder, with schoolmasters sometimes acting as middlemen. But the worst abuse is a situation whereby a young-ster is signed to a club so far from his home and school that it would be impossible to carry out the 'training and coaching' that are the whole purpose of the scheme.

What in fact such a club is doing is attemtping to get a lien on a promising player at an early age, and under the present regulations there is nothing to stop them doing that just. For just like professional players, associated schoolboys, that is kids of 13, 14 and 15, are registered by the Football League, and their registration cannot be transferred to another League club without the consent of the holding club – and this is fully spelt out in Rule 33 of the Football League.

If, therefore, the holding club do not offer the young boy a contract, he has no option but to wait a reasonable time, usually judged to be six months, before he can apply to join another club. At this stage in the boy's carreer, six months is a long time to have to wait before he can get back his freedom; but even more sinister is the fact that the club *can* sign the boy to apprentice forms within the six-month period, and once this is done the youngster is well and truly tied to the holding club, effectively for the rest of his playing life. For once he has signed as an apprentice, he cannot sign as a professional for another club without the consent of the holding club.

So from an early age, as young as thirteen, the accident of signing schoolboy forms for a particular club can determine the outcome of the young footballer's entire career. Obviously the majority of associated schoolboys and apprentices are happy with their clubs, but the wastage is enormous when you bear in mind that in an average league club only two players in the first team have usually come through the junior ranks. It would seem that clubs can exercise their options unscrupulously and hold on to an unwilling but possibly promising youngster, with the full backing of the regulations of the Football League.

The situation is much the same in the Scottish FA, though there is no apprentice scheme as such. Schoolboys may sign form 'S' as either amateur or professional, but on leaving school they cannot sign for any club other than the one to which they were attached as associate schoolboys, unless they are offered an apprenticeship contract within six months or are released by the holding club. If the youngster signs as an amateur, and elects to remain an amateur after leaving school, he cannot turn professional and join any club within the Scottish FA other than the one to which he was associated.

The Chester Committee came down heavily against the then regulations and recommended in para. 67 of their Report that the rules be amended, so that at the end of his period as an associated schoolboy, the youngster could sign apprentice forms with the club of his choice; this could in effect be the club with which he is associated, if he has been happy there and thinks he has had a fair deal. The committee added an important proviso, and this was that other clubs would not be allowed to approach the boy with offers until three months before the end of his attachment period.

Even at this stage when confronted with a disgruntled youngster clubs start talking about their investment in the boy. What this amounts to is doubtful and in any event they cannot reasonably expect to have all the options: to corner the market in talent; hold on to promising youngsters in case they might need them, and also have the right to drop them at a moment's notice if their talent does not mature. For no player at this stage receives any guarantee of employment.

APPRENTICESHIP

The next stage in the young footballer's career is the signing of apprenticeship forms. The apprentice scheme was introduced in 1960; before this date youngsters had been taken on as ground staff boys. The title may have changed but in some clubs the conditions have not, and apprentices find themselves with a number of chores to perform, including sweeping up the terraces and burning the rubbish after first-team games, scrubbing the dressing-room floor and cleaning the boots of the senior players. In between all this, they receive coaching and training, occasionally some form of further education and the amounts vary from club to club.

Apprentices are governed by Rule 47 of the Football League. Basically, an apprentice is a youngster of between 15 and 17, who has left school and is registered an as apprentice with a club. Apprenticeship terminates on his eighteenth birthday, but any time after his seventeenth birthday he may sign full professional forms. If he is still an apprentice at eighteen, he must either sign as a professional or revert to being an amateur. If he signs as a professional, this has to be to the holding club. If he becomes an amateur, he cannot sign for any other League club until two years have passed or he receives permission from the original club. The same situation applies if the apprentice applies for cancellation of his apprenticeship. This he can do if he feels the club is not honouring its obligations to him – for example by not letting him pursue further education or training for another job – and if permission is unreasonably withheld, he can appeal to the management committee of the Football League, and ultimately to the FA.

During his apprenticeship, the player receives a minimum wage at 15 to 16, rising when he reaches 17 and 18. The club can also help towards the apprentice's lodgings, up to an agreed maximum a week. And finally clubs cannot have more than fifteen apprentices on their books at any one time, though some clubs have got round this in the past by carrying a large number of young programme sellers or office boys on their staffs.

When the scheme was first introduced, returns from the League clubs showed 220 apprentices on their books, against 3,022 professionals, that is, a ratio of one apprentice for every 14 senior players. Six years later, the numbers had risen to nearly 600 apprentices against some 2,400 senior players, or one in four. Bearing in mind the abolition of the maximum wage in 1961, it is obvious that clubs had to cut down on their professional playing strength, sometimes, like Portsmouth, maintaining a squad of only twelve or fourteen first team players, and bolstering this with a pool of apprentices.

Apprentices can usefully bolster a club's reserve strength, but they cannot of course play in first team games until they have signed professional forms. But by maintaining a pool of apprentices, particularly above the age of seventeen, there is nothing to prevent a club from quickly offering professional forms to the youngster, to hastily patch up a first team depleted by injuries or transfers. And the temptation is for the boy to sign in haste, dazzled by the prospect of first team football, with no thoughts that he may be guaranteed a lasting place in the first team and without consideration of the financial benefits offered. A jump up from his £10 a week apprentice salary to double this figure may seem an attractive prospect, and if he were to accept the club would be buying him cheap.

THE CONTRACTED PROFESSIONAL

We have already seen how as an associated schoolboy, the young player is effectively tied to his club. The same is true when the end of his apprenticeship comes – he has two options: to sign for the holding club on whatever terms they offer; or get out of the game, because even if he reverts to his amateur status, he is effectively barred from playing for another League club for two years. Permission to transfer to another club may be given, but with strings: the holding club may demand some kind of (unreasonable) transfer fee, and thus in theory give their consent to a move but for all practical purposes hold on to the dissatisfied player.

The League went some way in 1967 when they introduced the transfer levy as a check on clubs unreasonably holding on to apprentices. This means that when an apprentice is signed as a professional, the club pays a fee of £500, half of which goes into the League's provident fund and half to the player. This is however a small sum for a large club able to maintain a pool of young professionals, who may not make the first team for several seasons, but are useful to keep on in case they command a transfer fee at some later stage.

Clubs argue against freedom of movement and point to their 'investment' in young players. Financially this does not amount to much. And training and coaching one extra boy cannot be said to make any difference. If the boy has no ability (according to the club) they should let him go and try somewhere else; or if he is good, then he should be free to settle with the club of his choice, whether this is the holding club or another. It is arguable how much coaching can improve his own natural ability and the Chester Committee again recommended that at this stage in the player's career he should be free to sign for any club.

The Chester Committee asked League clubs to supply them

F

with figures of apprentices. They received replies from thirty-seven clubs of the ninety-two (this alone is an interesting commentary on the interest some clubs take in football's wider issues), spread across the four divisions. Figures showed that 617 had joined the clubs during the previous five seasons Eighty-three had left the game altogether – a wastage of some 13 per cent. Three hundred had signed for their clubs (of these 222 were still with the same club, the other 78 had moved elsewhere).

What is most significant is that only 78 of those who had signed as professionals had played more than 10 times or more for the first team. And in the First Division (15 clubs replied), out of a pool of 165 first-team players, only 35 were former apprentices, i.e. *less than two players per team had come up through the scheme*. Yet it is the rich First Division clubs which can maintain the largest number of apprentices on their books.

It is clear then that apprenticeship is not the only way into football: clubs will continue to sign promising amateurs, players from minor non-League clubs and players from the second or third teams of large clubs will be transferred to smaller clubs, and so on. In fairness to the apprentices, they must be given training in a job outside football, and not be allowed to hang around the ground even in their spare time, or play pinball in the nearest café, a depressing sight all too often seen near football clubs. And no club should retain an unreasonably large apprentice squad as a means of cheap labour, to assist with ground cleaning: it is here that the FA could take a firmer action through its standing joint committee.

THE TRANSFER SYSTEM

However, it is when a full professional player moves from one club to another that we start to see all that is worst in the present transfer system. The season 1971–2 was something of a bonanza year for transfers, with 172 deals involving some £5½ million pounds in fees. Gone are the days of the mystical £100,000 transfer fee: out of the top twenty-four moves, half of these involved figures of £100,000 or more.

Topping the list were of course Everton's Alan Ball who went to Arsenal for £220,000 and David Nish's move to Derby. This was closely followed by the on-off-on deal involving Ian Moore's eventual move from Nottingham Forest to Manchester United for £200,000. Next in the race came west London idol Rodney Marsh, who quit Queens Park Rangers the day before the deadline and went to Manchester City for the same figure.

Crystal Palace sold their best forward Steve Kember to Chelsea (£170,000); Tony Green went from Blackpool to Newcastle (£150,000); Keith Weller moved north from Chelsea to Leicester (£100,000), following Alan Birchenal who had moved there from Crystal Palace for the same sum. Chelsea bought Chris Garland from Bristol City (£108,000). Even less-well-known names like Allan Hunter, who moved from Blackburn to Ipswich, commanded a £70,000 fee that hardly rated a headline. And so it went on.

Those who are in favour of retaining the present system argue that transfers are healthy for the game, bringing in much-needed revenue to smaller clubs, which develop their own home-grown starlets whom they eventually sell to a talent-hungry First Division club. But an examination of the total of moves inside the four divisions shows that this is simply not the case, as we shall see. First of all it is necessary to understand exactly what a transfer is.

Every player in England must be registered with the FA and with the Football League if he is employed by a League club. We have seen how this is the case even at the stage of being attached to a club as associated schoolboy or apprentice. The League scrutinizes contracts and may refuse a registration and it is the dash to St Annes on the Lancashire coast by harassed club secretaries to register a new signing that added to the (unnecessary) drama of the big-money signing.

The application for registration is made by the *club*, not by the player; so that registration is not so much a permit to play football as a permit to play football for a particular club. No player can be registered with two clubs at the same time, and movement from one club to another involves the transfer of the player's registration from the holding club to the signing club. Transfers have to be approved by both the FA and the League, and an application for a transfer must be signed by the player and both clubs – the one releasing him and the one who wants him. In simple terms, the holding club must agree to the transfer.

There, of course, is the rub, as a club can effectively hold on to a player who wants to move by means of a number of devices, some of them legal, forcing the player to appeal to the League to have his case for a move examined, some of them psychological – like putting the player 'on the list' but then blandly informing him that they have received no offers to buy. As most deals are initiated over the manager's ex-directory office telephone, it is hard for the player to prove anything in this situation and he must take the club's word for it, in spite of what he might read in the newspapers that 'manager X is interested in player Y'. Managers have a disarming habit of dismissing rumours of this kind, which are often planted by the club interested in buying the player, as 'paper talk'. Another device is to demand an unrealistic fee, clearly above what the player is worth, to frighten off interested clubs. The player can appeal against this and have the fee reduced, but the procedure is long and complicated and could take up to twelve months or more.

Obviously every player must have a contract with his club. This is a standard form, which sets out the terms and conditions of his employment: wages, bonuses for successes in the League or League or FA Cup competitions, and any other financial arrangements the player manages to wrest from the club at the time of signing. Contracts provide for an initial period followed by an option; the option being at the discretion of the club, and not being longer than the initial period. The normal arrangement is a 'one-plus-one' – one year certain, plus one year's option.

The option, however, is entirely on the club's side and once the player has signed he cannot move to another club without the holding club's permission, even at the end of the initial and option period. At this time the player has two choices (if he is refused a transfer): to sign on again with the holding club or get out of the game. This policy is endorsed by both the League and the FA and through their connections with the International Federation of Football Associations it virtually bars a player from joining a club outside his own country, if he decides to leave English football, as he will not be allowed to take part in any major competition.

Contracts are common in other professions, no less so in the entertainment industry. It is very very much an individual bargain – the performer agrees to give his exclusive services for a period of time in return for certain benefits and guarantees. The employer wishes to secure the talents of the performer, for a fixed period, but runs the risk that these may deteriorate – long contracts are said to be the reason why some performers remain on our television screens long after they have lost popularity with the public.

The performer for his part runs the risk of tying himself to an employer who may not exploit him fully and if he is in doubt he may look for a shorter-term contract, which can be re-negotiated at the end of the contract period if both parrties wish to continue the arrangement. If he opts for security of employment, he will ask for a longer contract. And so on. The footballer, however, is in the unique position of being tied for ever, possibly, to his employer.

In 1963 the arrangements for renewing a player's contract were changed, as a result of the George Eastham case (see p. 60). Before 1963 a player registered with a club could find himself at the end of his contract period in one of four situations. His contract was renewed – fine if he could negotiate satis-factory terms and conditions for himself. Or he could be retained by the club – even at a wage lower than his existing wage (i.e. a first team player who is getting on, but the club thought he would be useful to them in the reserves). If the player refused to accept the new deal and no other club was prepared to buy him (and remember it is the selling club that nominates the price), the player could be retained indefinitely by the holding club, neither under contract nor allowed to sign for another club, clearly an iniquitous situation.

The third course of action was for the player to be placed on the transfer list and the holding club was under no obligation at this stage to continue paying him wages! If, however, he accepted even the minimum wage, he could not sign for a non-League club. If he was not paid, he could join such a club – tantamount to quitting the professional game altogether.

If none of the three situations arose, the player was free to leave of his own accord.

As a result of the Eastham case the rules were changed and the situation now is this: if a club wishes to retain a player at the end of the contract or option period, they offer him new terms and the player has four weeks in which to decide whether he accepts them or not. All players have to be informed at the end of the playing season whether the club proposes to retain them or put them on the transfer list. If a player is on neither list, then he can sign for another club.

The player the club wishes to retain then decides and if he has not re-signed at the latest by 30 June, he is regarded as in dispute with his club. Until the dispute is resolved by appealing to the management committee of the League or ultimately the independent tribunal, the player is retained by the holding club on the same wage as his old contract, and continues to play for them.

The independent tribunal must adjudicate by the end of the following September, well into the new season, and if they decide in the club's favour, the player may still refuse their verdict and continue to play for the club on his old contract, while continuing to press for a transfer. It is at this stage that astute managers put players up for sale at an unrealistically high fee or deny that offers are being received for the player, who has then to seek the support of his union and continue to press for another hearing.

All that the independent tribunal can do is decide whether the terms offered by the club are fair or not – they cannot oblige the club to release the dissatisfied player. Later, they can decide that the transfer fee asked is too high and have it reduced.

Obviously the longer the player is in dispute with his club

and unable to get away, the less are his chances of finding a new club: for example, a club might go shopping for a particular type of player and when the one they want is not available they will fill the gap with someone else, and the player in dispute has lost his chance of a good move.

Most free transfers occur in the Third and Fourth Divisions, and generally between 15 per cent and 20 per cent of players are on the move at the end of any one season, for free.

But most transfers are for money and as we have seen the season 1971–2 was no exception. Players are generally moved around in the middle of their contract period, and the price asked reflects the selling club's reluctance to part with their man, coupled with the keenness or desperation of the buying club. Those in favour of the system argue that the money stays in the game – London Weekend's Brian Moore made this statement commenting on the Ian Moore and Rodney Marsh transfers in March 1971. They also argue that financially worse off clubs can benefit from the system, and for many years pointed to Burnley which survived in the First Division until 1971 on the strength of ability to bring up promising youngsters of their own and then sell them to richer clubs.

The Chester Committee went into the figures very thoroughly and their analysis showed clearly that the process of transfers is downwards rather than upwards, that is, First and Second Division clubs selling to Third and Fourth Division clubs, and *not* the other way round. According to figures supplied by the PFA, of 1,488 transfers within the League during the period under review, 848 were from higher divisions to lower, and only 206 from lower divisions upwards. By far the largest majority of these players left the First Division, to join clubs in the Second and Third.

What tends to obscure the situation is that when there is a movement upward – say, Chris Garland from Bristol City to Chelsea – the size of the transfer fee seems to show that money is going from the senior clubs to help smaller clubs. This simply is not so. Most of the large fees are in fact paid by one First Division club to another, or less often by a Second Division club to a First – and generally the Second Division club has recently

been in the First Division and is trying to get back there. During
1971–2 none of the top two dozen transfers over the £60,000
figure were from Third or Fourth Division clubs; and only
eight were from the Second Division.

It used to be argued that the lower divisions were the
nurseries of the top clubs and that as a result money flowed from
the top to the bottom. This is now simply not the case. First
Division and other clubs all have their own network of talent
scouts, and by using the associated schoolboy and apprentice
systems, it is unlikely that promising youngsters slip through
it. Top clubs attract the best youngsters, who want the glamour
of playing for Leeds or Manchester United. If things do not
work out, the player's value is enhanced by association with the
larger club and he can transfer downwards for a good fee.

In the lower divisions it is hard for a player to attract attention, and therefore offers, unless he is a spectacular goal
scorer. Such a man was Ted McDougall of lowly Bournemouth.

To sum up: the large clubs survive on their own resources,
drawing on their second team and reserve squads. They go
shopping only when a crisis situation demands the purchase of
a particular player for a special job – a goalkeeper or a striker,
for example. Most of the expensive buys are either from other
First Division clubs or from outside the Football League,
notably of course from Scotland. By contrast, clubs in the
lower divisions, while developing their own talent, are often
unable to retain their best youngsters who want to move on and
upwards, and so they have to replace them from the First and
Second Divisions; purchase figures are lower, but the sum
total of deals is quite spectacular.

Contracts are obviously necessary – to bind players to a club
for a certain time and enable the club to get and hold together
a first team squad. But at the end of the contract period, say
one year, the option to renew is on the club's side only; and at
the end of the option period, say a further year, then again the
option is with the club. Players know the rules, it is argued,
when they sign in the first place, but then they have no choice if
they wish to stay in top-class football, as these arrangements are
endorsed by the League and FA collectively. True there are

rights of appeal, eventually, and a clearly unhappy player is no use to his club: this will be reflected in his play and performance. But you do hear of players apparently trying to get away from their clubs, and examples that come to mind include Arsenal's Peter Marinello and Alun Evans of Liverpool.

Troubled by the contract situation, the Chester Committee over *five years ago* recommended that contracts between a player and his club should automatically cease, once the contract period had ended; and that transfer fees should not be paid, unless a player's contract was purchased in mid-term, i.e. before it had run its time. Cries went up in Lytham and Lancaster Gate that this would not work, but I think it would.

Imagine the situation: a club signs a player whom they wish to keep, so they try and go for a longish contract, four, five or seven years. The player for his part can opt for security and agree to sign, bearing in mind that the club might go through a bad patch and drop into a lower division or other circumstances might prejudice his playing career. The club runs the risk that the player might lose form or suffer an injury. So both sides have something to gain, something to lose when negotiating the contract, which would truly be a free bargain struck between two equal parties.

Imagine the situation at the end of the contract period: both sides are free to part, but obviously a player may be happy to stay with his club and be willing to sign on for another period. And the club may be anxious to retain him, and will make their terms for doing so at least as attractive as the offers the player may be receiving from rival clubs. And again another bargain would be freely struck between the two sides.

The League and the FA have long argued that transfer fees are in fact payments for a release from contract – but it is hard to justify this argument when clubs sell players whom they do not wish to retain and who have fulfilled their contract period for their club. It is plain money-grubbing, and only enforceable because of the monopoly position of the League and FA.

The new system would bring dignity into the transfer system and it is doubtful whether there would be any more movement between clubs than there is at present. As we said earlier, players may be happy to stay with their clubs for professional, social and business reasons: if they are happy with the club's progress in the League and competitions, if they have married and settled down locally, and have personal or business ties with the area. And even if it is every player's dream to turn out for Manchester United, that eminent club cannot possibly take all the best forwards or defenders in the League, for clearly economic and practical reasons. So the system would find its own level.

Transfer fees could still be paid if a club wished to acquire a player who still had some time to run on his contract with his holding club – for example, a club that had lost its top scorer might be forced to find a replacement half way through the season to keep up their position in the League table or to avoid relegation. The new system would mean that a player's contract would be valued according to how long it had to run – its value being nil at the end of the contract period, as neither party is under obligation to the other. So a fee paid for a player would reflect this, it would be some kind of compensation for depriving the club of the benefits of the contract with its player. And an interested club might decide to wait until nearly the end of the player's contract before deciding to approach him, to offer better terms than those proposed by the club he is with. And we would get a free transfer situation as outlined above. It would be up to the holding club then to counter this offer with a better one, if they wished to retain their man.

With regard to transfer from Scotland into English League football, some adjustment might have to be made, such as restricting free transfers to within the Football League only. Scottish clubs rely heavily on fees received for players sold to clubs south of the border, and it might be unfair for Scottish players to be able to move freely out of Scottish football into the English League without their club receiving anything for them. Special rates could perhaps be worked out.

The same might apply to transfers between other countries – that is, the case of a player who leaves an English club to join an Italian club at the end of his contract period. He then wishes to rejoin an English club, and the Italians could demand a large fee. Something would have to be worked out with FIFA to cover transfers between different countries.

So far the League and FA have failed to act on this recommendation of the Chester Committee, though as recently as March 1972 Cliff Lloyd, secretary of the Professional Footballers Association, suggested again that the system could work and put forward a five-point plan outlining his ideas.

The present system has clearly got out of hand, when one examines the huge sums involved. And at a lower level, a lot of hardship is unnecessarily inflicted on players retained by their clubs.

Chapter 6

Football and the Media

Professional football feeds a wealth of news, comment and gossip to the media. Every national and regional paper carries its sports pages and both BBC and ITV feature major sports programmes on Saturday or Sunday every week. In addition there is a host of football magazines published weekly or monthly. If the media live off football, it is true that football owes a lot to the media: but the relationship is far from being an easy one. We shall examine why.

Like footballers, sports writers have never quite made it socially. This is probably only true of this country, where sports news is invariably confined to the back pages of newspapers and there is no really serious sports magazine that can be bought and enjoyed by an intelligent adult readership.

The sports pages fall into several categories: those of the national newspapers which concentrate on major First Division games, build-up stories for big matches, Cup Finals and European competitions. They produce regionalized coverage of important local games, so that the sports section of the *Daily Express* you buy in Exeter in no way resembles the copy you read in Hull.

The Sunday newspapers follow the same pattern, carrying reports of the previous day's games and gossip sections like Sam Bartram's column in *The People* or Ken Montgomery in the *Sunday Mirror*. These titbits, instantly forgettable and culled from rumours and dressing-room gossip, range from transfer hints to details of players' suspensions and fines.

Footballers and/or managers themselves often deny what is in them, dismissing the comments as 'paper talk', but occasionally use them to plant stories about unrest or a manager's supposed interest in a player from another club, in order to get a transfer proposition rolling. A player who openly asks for a move loses his 5 per cent of the transfer fee: much more discreet to get a friendly journalist to hint in his column that he would not refuse a move to another club. Honour and cash are saved all round.

Further down the scale you get the regional and local newspapers. They can include important regional dailies like the *Northern Echo* or *Western Daily Press*, published in the mornings in Middlesbrough and Cardiff respectively, or lively evening newspapers like the *Yorkshire Evening Post* (Leeds) or the *Brighton Evening Argus*. There are also peripheral suburban weeklies in London, so that for detailed coverage of Crystal Palace you reach for the *Croydon Advertiser* or for Millwall the *South-East London Mercury*.

Reporters on these newspapers often enjoy a close relationship with the club, being on christian name terms with players, the manager and directors. Often a privileged journalist will travel to away games in the team coach. The problem is that they either become cynical and disenchanted about the club's performances, or still continue to write more or less inoffensively about the team's misfortunes. Often they do what is virtually a public relations job for the club, explaining to their readership the management line on why a certain player cannot be bought or building of the new stand has to be delayed for yet another season.

The closeness of the relationship is something that is both closely guarded and also rarely acknowledged. Reporters who have covered the same club for many years tend to develop a hard-baked 'I've seen it all before attitude' and the press box at relatively unimportant Second Division games really does throw up the stock cartoon image of the journalist, complete with soiled raincoat and greasy trilby hat. It is not an inspiring sight and newcomers are not welcome.

There is ill-disguised rivalry with the nationals and the arrival of the man from the *Mirror* or the *Express* to cover an important Cup game can put a strain on tempers and physical resources in an overcrowded press box.

Shuffling along behind the commentators and reporters come the writers for the weekly and monthly football magazines. Not quite accepted by football clubs or their fellow journalists, they seem themselves to be acutely conscious of their inferior status, aware that what they write does not carry the urgency and immediacy of a national press report.

Football magazines have to rely heavily on gossip and background material, and what you read one week is much the same as last week and the week before: only the names have been changed. It is surprising that in spite of all the sports activity which exists this country does not support a daily sports newspaper like the French *L'Equipe*. Consequently, with mid-week deadlines, the magazines invariably miss out on the really hard news, and retain a young and fairly illiterate readership by means of fan pictures and bland first-person pieces like 'Full backs I fear most' or 'United really can make it', ghost written by disillusioned hacks.

The pity is that the magazines are in a unique position to explore and expose some of the wider issues of football and the fact they do not is one of the reasons why this book is being written. So much could be said that is not being said. There are arguments that there is no readership for this kind of more serious football reporting, that the job of the press is to inform and entertain, not persuade or campaign. There is also the problem of libel, though there is no case on record of a footballer suing a reporter because he wrote that the player performed badly, but presumably it could happen.

Most of the football magazines get involved in the 'annual game', producing glossy rehashes of the previous season's pictures, and spotting the books with first-person pieces, club surveys and star interviews. One year I counted some twenty-five of these publications; by the second year the number had doubled and in the third year the figure was nearer eighty. Clearly the market has a struggle to absorb all of these, as they are bought primarily by youngsters with limited pocket money.

'They like big pictures', one publisher insisted, 'so that they can collect the player's autograph outside the dressing-room'. Another one instructed 'Include a chapter on Blackpool, we have a good wholesaler there'.

Unfortunately too many publishers climbed on the annual bandwagon shortly after the 1966 World Cup and too many books were produced too cheaply. The result was that the market was saturated, sales overall were low, and firms lost money. One disappointing book will affect sales of the others, as kids are not as gullible as some publishers would have us believe.

Jimmy Hill and Brian Moore are probably the best known television personalities. Moore received added exposure through his job as link man during ITV's coverage of the 1972 Olympics. In the spring of 1973, Hill moved to the BBC from London Weekend Television, joining an already formidable array of sports experts that include ex-*Sunday Mirror* man Sam Leitch, Barry Davies (another refugee from commercial TV), Frank Bough and David Coleman, thus leaving Moore and Dickie Davies to hold together the entire ITV sports department.

Both channels run football magazine programmes. ITV have their *On the Ball* spot around one o'clock on Saturday afternoon, at the start of their sports coverage. This is confidently handled by Moore, originally televised live at the ground from which the match was to be recorded later on. Half the fun is in trying to guess which! BBC carry their *Match of the Day* programme on Saturday evening, with Barry Davies as link-man. ITV reply with *The Big Match* on Sunday afternoon.

All the programmes present much the same mixture: news and gossip, interviews with players and managers, bother before and after matches, and a brief look at European football. Both have competitions like 'Goal of the Month' or 'Penalty Prize'. ITV scored with Jimmy Hill. His match analyses were convincingly done and one got the impression that both he and Moore felt at home among professional footballers and knew what they were talking about. By contrast the BBC give the impression that they are televising football when they really should be putting out ballet or show jumping, and infuriating viewers with their over-use of the ubiquitous action replay.

A newcomer on the scene was BBCs supposedly 'serious' sports programme put out on BBC-2 on Thursdays and hosted by actor/writer Colin Welland and Ian Wooldridge, a sports writer with the *Daily Mail*. Both men tried too hard to stamp their personalities on the programme, which lost as a result.

Like the magazines and the daily press, television tends to dodge the real issues and concentrates instead on trivia. True, Jimmy Hill has unswervingly supported the crackdown on violence on the field and has been a champion in the cause of 'total football'. But the real, personal issues are avoided. There is no excuse for this. Unlike the journalist from the local paper, television commentators do not have to rely on maintaining good relations with a club or particular players. They should use their freedom and their prestige to be more outspoken and occasionally say something constructive about football in the wider sense.

To Hill's credit one must mention his unflinching attack on the Manchester United board at the time of the George Best/ Frank O'Farrell crisis. In an amazing 'open letter to the United board' broadcast in London Weekend's sports programme on Saturday 16 December – a few hours before the club's ignominious defeat at Crystal Palace – he criticized the board for their handling of the affair and forcing manager Frank O'Farrell into a position where he was almost bound to resign. Hill endorsed his views the following day while commenting on the televised broadcast of the match.

Even television match commentaries are models of innocuous uniformity. Moves are rarely criticized or commented on. It can be argued that the commentator should say as little as possible and let the game speak for itself, but anyone who has stood in a football crowd knows that spectators like to analyse and argue about the state of play, and no one watches football passively. If only someone would occasionally say something provocative.

MATCH REPORTING

Reporting the Saturday afternoon or mid-week evening game is undertaken by a variety of full- and part-time sports journalists. The regional and local papers have their regular man, at home and away games. Every national newspaper has two or three name sports writers, who between them cover the top First Division games or occasionally descend on a lowlier club to cover an important League Cup or FA Cup match involving a First Division side. Typically, Hereford, still in the Southern League in 1971-2, received a mass visitation from the nationals for their game against West Ham in the fourth round of the FA Cup.

Less important games, from the Second Division downwards, are covered by part-time reporters or stringers, who travel away each Saturday for a fixed fee and expenses. Occasionally, a national paper will take a report from a local man on the spot, who operates a sort of agency service supplying sports news for a number of papers.

Match coverage is essentially a question of timing. On a Saturday afternoon, reporters covering the game for evening papers telephone or are telephoned by their offices every fifteen minutes, and the commentary is dictated to a copy-taker almost as it happens. The final report is wrapped up within minutes of the final whistle, and what has been said is set in type, printed and on the streets in the 'classified' or green or pink editions by five-thirty or six o'clock, carrying full match reports and final scores of all the afternoon's League games.

An evening match will present similar problems of timing for national papers. With a seven-thirty kick-off, an evening match should end by nine-fifteen, giving reporters fifteen or twenty minutes to compose and phone through their pieces. Some nationals print in both London and Manchester, but even so some regional editions for the West Country or the far north have to be printed and put on board scheduled trains at Paddington or Euston soon after 10 or 11 p.m. Reporters then usually compose another piece for the Midland and Home Counties editions and the London papers.

A last-minute goal or sudden reversal of fortunes can alter the whole character of a piece, involving an entire rewrite at the end of the match, and only a few minutes can be allowed for this. There may be bonus news items as well – a bomb threat at Orient or the tragedy at Ibrox as the spectators left the pitch.

Photographers sitting on the goal line hope for an early score – at their end of the pitch. A London newspaper will usually cover the opponents' goal, in order to get a picture of the home side scoring. Rolls of film are then handed to despatch riders who race them to Fleet Street for developing and processing, so that the blocks can be made and pictures printed for the classified editions – often earlier.

Newspapers also collect library shots of individual players, particularly new signings, so that they have on file an up-to-date picture of a player in his new team strip. These are taken in the few minutes before kick-off, when the two teams run on to the pitch for a few minutes' kick-around before the game starts.

Having despatched their preliminary match report, some journalists like to, or are obliged to, amplify this with background information or quotes from managers and players. Some managers are co-operative about this, understanding the needs of the press. Bert Head of Crystal Palace always used to come up to the press room within ten or fifteen minutes of the game ending, to answer reporters' questions or offer a few comments. These sometimes make headlines like 'We were diabolical' says Head.

Playere are harder to pin down, as it is not always easy to penetrate the dressing-room. Professional footballers are on the whole suspicious of pressmen and are not necessarily articulate. It is sometimes difficult to drag from them anything more than the standard clichés, 'The ball just happened to be there and I kicked it into the net', or 'All the lads played well really and we're looking forward to playing United next week'. It is often necessary to put words into the player's mouth by careful phrasing of questions. Players rarely resent this – they are happy to appear intelligent – and although they will not admit it to a reporter they read every word said about them. After away matches there is a rush to buy the local sporting edition at the station kiosk before boarding the train for home, and players spend a large part of the journey analysing and discussing newspaper reports, sensitive if they are mentioned critically and ribbing each other if they have earned praise for their performance.

Most top-line reporters will expect to be on good terms with three or four players from each First Division club, and their pocket book of players' private telephone numbers is part of their stock in trade. These are the people they can telephone for quotes and comments, or whom they can tap for inside information about a transfer rumour or pay dispute. Whether players receive payment for this kind of service is hard to say – no one admits it. Paying footballers for first-person and interview pieces is a practice that was started by the football magazines, and spread to newspapers and radio and television interviews. I have not in my experience come across a player who did not want paying for an interview and one First Division footballer once stopped me in mid-sentence over the telephone to ask, 'By the way, is there anything in it for me. . . .'

A Cup Final run is a bonanza time for players, and the price accordingly goes up. Money from interviews and articles goes into a pool, divided among the first-team squad, though some players have contracts with particular newspapers.

Some papers disdain to indulge in dressing-room gossip, and it is the popular tabloids which run columns like 'Sportlight' (*Daily Mirror*) or Sam Bartram's in *The People*. *The Times*, *Sunday Times*, *Observer* and *Telegraph* tend to report matches in much the same way as they review theatre or music: they do this without interviewing the performers. This tends to give their match reports a certain air of remoteness, with references like Charlton, R. when we all know the player as Bobby Charlton.

It is the quality newspapers however which have developed the name sports writers. These men are the elite of their profession and are often not employed directly by the paper, but work on contract or have a loose arrangement with them that allows participation in radio or television, magazines and books. Football writers tend to suffer some kind of inferiority complex about their work, and are anxious to prove themselves in other spheres. They do not have the prestige of the arts critics or the specialists in industry or finance. Part of the reason for this may be because the sports pages, tucked away at the back of the paper or hidden in the middle, do not attract much advertising revenue; there is no such thing as a male market, in the way that a product can be launched to appeal to all women.

So the sports pages rely heavily on advertising from the pools companies or big bookmakers, and the football magazines on manufacturers of sports gear – boots, strip etc. – or fan requirements – records, scrapbooks, programmes, football annuals and so on.

The Sunday papers carry the most prestigious football writers. They include Brian Glanville of *The Sunday Times*; Tony Pawson of *The Observer*; Danny Blanchflower of the *Sunday Express*. They are football's elite of intellectuals, but how seriously they are taken is a matter for conjecture. More down to earth are Norman Giller of the *Daily Express*, Ian Wooldridge of the *Daily Mail*, Ken Jones of the *Mirror*, and Victor Railton of the London *Evening News*. The *Evening Standard* has two elder statesmen in the shape of Bernard Joy (a formal Arsenal player) and sports columnist J. L. Manning.

The sports columnists form a super-elite even amongst this select group of writers, and as well as Manning include Wooldridge of the *Mail*, Michael Parkinson (*Sunday Times*, *Punch* and elsewhere), Hugh McIlvanney (ex *Observer* and now *Daily Express*), and Arthur Hopcraft (author and playwright).

A number of these writers have entered other fields, Glanville as author of several novels, Hopcraft as a writer on general topics and Parkinson as a TV personality hosting his own chat show on BBC and before that discussing films for Granada. The reasons for this diversification, I suspect, include pursuit of something more intellectually satisfying than sports reporting and frustration at the narrow specialization of the paper's sports department. It is hard to make a transition to any other section of the newspaper, and even sport is divided into specialist areas: a racing man would never cover a football match. Once a writer is known as a sports specialist it is difficult to make the transition to more general writing though the techniques of interviewing and assessment could reasonably be applied in another area.

A recent trend has been the employment of outsiders to head a name column, like former Manchester City manager Joe Mercer in the *Daily Mail* or the *Evening Standard*'s pieces by a player from each of the London clubs several evenings a week. The players' pieces are often ghost-written, and a small-type reference is made to the journalist involved. The practice can get out of hand and some journalists resent the fact that players can be paid more than the writers for lending their name to such columns. Whether the public believes the footballer actually wrote the piece is a debatable point.

The football magazines have carried this practice to the extreme. The weekly *Goal* sports Bobby Charlton's diary and the ubiquitous George Best pops up again in *Shoot*, a colourful tabloid aimed at younger football fans.

I have myself interviewed some two hundred professional players in the course of preparing various books and articles. It is not an easy job to recall the background and playing highlights of the man's career, which makes a lot of interviews hard going. Often a long and involved question will elicit little reaction. I recall once asking an international player something like: 'Before the World Cup, there were criticisms in the press that your style of play had been inhibited by playing alongside Hurst and Moore, yet after Mexico you seemed to acquire more confidence in your own ability to score rather than make goals. Would you say this was true?'. The player: 'Yes'.

With a two-thousand-word deadline, this sort of answer does not make life easy for the sports writer. There is also the question of how much of a footballer's off-the-field activities should constitute news: does the player deserve a private life? Often this is denied him, and George Best's latest escapade or the wedding of a prominent footballer or the odd drunken driving case will be classed as *news* and escape from the sports page to appear at the front of the paper.

Off the field footballers are quite often not very interesting to talk to, and many even are painfully shy of discussing their sport. So the need to fill column inches results in chatty pieces about their cars or their clothes, their wives or girlfriends.

FOOTBALL MAGAZINES

This cult of the football personality is particularly found in the tabloids and the football magazines. If you look through a year's issues of either *Goal* or *Shoot*, you see the same old names. Currently they favour Rodney Marsh, Tony Currie, Kevin Keegan, Colin Bell, Colin Todd, Alan Hudson, Alan Ball, Mick Channon, Trevor Hockey, Martin Peters. Just a handful of players out of two thousand professionals.

A more serious attempt at covering football's wider issues was made in a Marshall Cavendish part work *Book of Football*. This was not a bad try, and the content included a look at football economics, profiles of all the League clubs and some non-League, sensible profiles of players and managers, and occasional pieces on the press, football programmes, history of the FA Cup and so on. Unfortunately part works generally have had a hard time of it lately, and suffer from being written so far in advance of publication that they can scarcely be called topical.

Goal announces itself as 'the world's greatest soccer weekly' and enjoys the largest circulation. It is edited by portly Alan Hughes, a former Fleet Street man, and contributors – in name at least – include Bobby Charlton. Ken Jones of the *Daily Mirror* also writes, and BBC Television's Jimmy Hill tackles a current issue every week. With a line-up like that it should be good, but of its fifty odd pages half are taken up with full-page pictures of players or teams, or with advertising. It is the sort of magazine you can read from cover to cover without actually learning anything, and too many of the articles fail because of their innocuousness. A typical issue in August 1972 included the following headlines: 'This Ball is worth £300,000 –

Alan gets the Arsenal machine bubbling again'; 'Peter Shilton is back on top'; 'I'm happy to keep my Chelsea place, says goal-a-game Garland'; or 'We're going to have a great season – Dobing' – hardly calculated to set the nerves tingling.

Shoot costs 6p and reaches, presumably, a younger audience. A May 1972 issue of forty pages had twelve whole-page pictures and numerous others scattered throughout the text. Editor is David Gregory, and the contents include 'George Best's Diary' and 'Bobby Moore writes for You' – that week it was the hoary old standby, a piece about the England squad in training and what a jolly time they all have with Uncle Alf Ramsey. Arsenal's Alan Ball also contributes 'Soccer as I see it' and each week a player replies to readers' letters in matey man-to-boy fashion. The feature 'Crosstalk' is an interesting item, a sort of dialogue between players on a football topic, and that week it was Colin Bell (Manchester City) and Keith Weller (Leicester) talking about the responsibilities of being team captain. There is also a useful weekly club survey.

Inside Football (incorporating *Striker*) is printed in tabloid newspaper format but carries little hard news. The mixture is depressingly very much as before – 'Rangers lose Marsh shadow' or 'Willie the Wisp Anderson keeps Villa on the move'. There is another club-by-club survey, three pages of pools information, quizzes, and mini-profiles of new or up and coming players. It is hard to discern a conscious editorial policy in the paper, a fault that is common to the other two weeklies as well.

The two controlling football bodies publish their own propaganda sheets in the shape of the *FA News* (monthly) and the *Football League Review* (more or less weekly and given away at certain clubs with the football programme).

The Football Association News is published commercially and in addition to the editor has a Football Association advisory committee of four people, including secretary Denis Follows. In the September 1972 issue of forty-six pages, twenty-one were made up of advertisements or pictures. Again there is no conscious direction in the publication. Admittedly, England team manager Sir Alf Ramsey contributes a piece on 'England's

World Cup Prospects: A halftime Report' and Denis Follows analyses the findings of the Wheatley Report on crowd safety. But again the same banal headings appear: 'Leeds can top the Table' (Reg Drury, of the *News of the World*); a profile of Leeds player Norman Hunter by Bernard Joy of the *Evening Standard*; a piece on Tottenham 'Always Looking Forward – that's Spurs'; a piece about the work of the St Johns' Ambulance Brigade; and a feature on floodlighting, heavily supported by advertising from the various manufacturers.

The *Football League Review* – managing editor and public relations officer Alan Hardaker – is programme size and more chatty in style: we're just one big happy family is the message. A twenty-four-page issue I examined contained nearly twelve pages of pictures and advertisements, and topics covered included a piece by Hardaker on the new points plan for discipline; a review of the Anglo-Italian tournament; readers' letters; and the remainder made up of snippets about individual players or clubs. It reads very much like a poorly edited football programme.

Their affairs conducted at a more leisurely pace, the monthlies, one would hope would go some of the way towards looking at football in greater depth. Unfortunately this is not the case. I examined three publications: *Monthly Football*, *Football Pictorial* and *Sportsworld*. The last named used to call itself *World Sports* and covers other sports besides soccer.

Monthly Football is a glossy affair, with seventy-odd pages and is edited by Pat Collins. Pictures and advertisements accounted for some forty-five pages – a very high ratio – and the articles have a certain familiarity about them: 'It must be Chelsea . . .' 'Head gets busy' or 'Schoolmaster put me on road to top'. The quality of the picture reproduction is better than most and there is a useful coaching section, by Crystal Palace manager Malcolm Allison. Another ray of hope was – in the issue I looked at – an article about players on loan and suggested a time limit of six weeks for such transactions.

Football Pictorial is the official journal of the Federation of Football Supporters' Clubs, an organization founded by Tony Pullein. The magazine is printed on a mixture of coated and rag paper, and the forty-eight-page issue I examined carried twenty-five pages of photographs and four more of line drawings of players, leaving just eighteen or nineteen pages of text. Sample article headings included 'Kember can clip critics', 'Midefild power should revive Everton', and 'We're stepping up in grade' (about players newly signed for Bournemouth).

By contrast, *Sportsworld* is a curious mixture. The magazine likes to think it is a bit outrageous: they once printed an interview with boxer Chris Finnegan in which he said he counted the minutes before he could indulge in sex again, after a professional bout. The hefty seventy-page issue I looked at had some thirty-seven pages of pictures or advertisements, including ing an extra pull-out section on Munich 1972. Most of the issue was devoted to the Olympics and sensibly, soccer being in its close season, the editors had not tried to create football news for the sake of filling the pages.

One interesting innovation in the magazine field was *Football Academy*, a magazine that attempted to pass on football skills by means of analysis, pictures and diagrams. One issue I examined had Orient manager George Petchey on the role of centre backs; Allen Wade, director of coaching for the FA, on triangle formations; Tom McNab, an AAA national coach, on fitness; Leicester City's Peter Shilton on goalkeeping techniques; and articles on the laws of football, dribbling the ball, running and hints from several coaches and players. The design and layout of the magazine are good and no advertising is carried.

For those who listen, BBC radio continues to put out a fair amounts of sports coverage. On Saturday afternoons, this consists of, usually, the second-half coverage of a League match, but the main focus of attention is the 5 p.m. programme *Sports Report*, currently produced by Bob Burrows. This is anything up to an hour long, and includes the classified results, comments on the afternoon's football, interviews with players and managers.

It is doubtful whether anyone can ever make it to the top as a radio sports journalist, though names that come to mind are those of presenters Peter Jones and Desmond Lynam.

CRITICISMS

A look at the media in relation to football suggests there are three main criticisms: the concentration on trivialities, which we have examined in the magazines and popular newspapers; the absence of top-class sports writers; and the encroachment of players and managers into highly paid contracts in journalism.

The lack of serious coverage of football and its wider issues seems to suggest that editors and publishers think that the football public is only intelligent enough to appreciate this sort of stuff. Here I think they are wrong. The *Sun* and *Daily Mirror* have two of the highest national newspaper circulations and the standard of journalism is first class – not least in the ill-fated *Mirror Magazine*, a rival to the heavy colour supplements, that came and went with some rapidity.

Yet if you can find a John Pilger or a Monty Meth on the news pages and columnists of the appeal of Marjorie Proops, why should it be so difficult to blossom on the sports pages?

In October 1972 the *Mirror* lost one of its most famous sports columnists, Peter Wilson. A former public schoolboy, Wilson became famous during the fifties for his campaign to remove the colour bar in boxing. At the time he was labelled 'the man they cannot gag' and wrote some of the most entertaining prose on sports as widely differing as boxing and lawn tennis.

Sadly it is left to the heavies to breed articulate sports writers, but football followers tend not to be readers of *The Observer* and *The Sunday Times*. Nor are these papers purchased for the quality of their sports coverage. While the football magazines concentrate on an essentially young readership, there is clearly a need for a serious adult sports magazine.

Akin to the publication of football trivia is the growing practice of using 'star' names to attract a flagging readership. This is most evident in the big-name series popular with certain Sunday papers, when a player or manager reveals all in a two- or three-part series. Brian Clough did this and eventually won himself a lasting place in the *Sunday Express*.

Around Cup Final time the scramble for top names and exclusive pieces reaches frantic proportions, as the newspapers vie

with one another for a scoop. Players form themselves into a
pool or appoint an agent to sort out the offers from the press and
television and the whole process can degenerate into an undig-
nified auction. It is traditional at this time to play off the BBC
against ITV for the privilege of filming interviews and stories to
be used during the pre-match build-up on Cup Final day.

Some literary agents specialize in commissioning auto-
biographies of players and if there is anything the least bit
sensational in the resulting manuscript parts of it can be sold,
reputedly for high sums, to one of the Sunday papers. This
process is often necessary in order to recoup the cash outlay on a
book, which includes payments to the footballer and his ghost-
writer. It is doubtful however whether editors will continue to
lay out huge sums for football exclusive when there is no
guarantee that they will add a single new reader to their
circulation figures.

Substantial payments of this kind to sportsmen make a
mockery of serious journalism and writers are doing themselves
a disservice when they allow their names to be appended to a
ghost-written column – 'Player X was talking to reporter Y'.
The money paid out cannot be significant to a footballer who is
already in the surtax bracket and the practice is bound to
undermine the professional working relationship between
reporters and sportsmen.

It is arguable too whether the reading public is taken in by
this sort of thing. They realize all too easily that footballers
are not necessarily articulate and certainly few are capable of
putting together a well-balanced newspaper piece. So no one
reading the column really believes it comes from the mouth of
the player concerned. Editors may be able to get away with this
sort of thing on smaller provincial papers, where as we have seen
the reporter's relationship with the football club is a more
intimate one. On the whole however the practice seems to
suggest that editors regard their readers as both unintelligent
and gullible.

Chapter 7

The Players:
Some Typical Problems

What then of the stalwart young men who make up the playing staffs of the ninety-two League clubs? A quick count at the start of the 1972–3 season revealed some nineteen hundred 'first team' players spread across the four Divisions, with 590 in the First Division, 500 in the Second, 420 in the Third and 360 in the Fourth. One must bear in mind that the Third and Fourth Divisions each have twenty-four clubs, as against twenty-two each in the First and Second.

Attention has already been drawn to the varying sizes of first-team squads; most First Division clubs average between twenty and thirty players in this category. There is a slight reduction in the Second Division, some clubs, newly relegated from the First for example, carrying with them the legacy of better days. Squads are much reduced in the lower Divisions, averaging twenty first team players or less – Brentford, Port Vale and Tranmere Rovers listed only thirteen apiece. And down in the Fourth squads are tinier still, invariably under twenty (except for Barnsley, newly relegated to the Fourth Division), and one club, Crewe Alexandra, listed only seven first-team players at the time of writing!

A player's success in his profession will depend on a number of factors, not least of which is of course his own ability. Talent will on the whole find its level and the skilful player, even if he starts his career in a lowly side, will quickly move up into one of the higher Divisions. His original club will not be able to keep him, and they will welcome the money they can get by selling his registration to a Second or First Division club.

There is also an element of luck, being born in a football catchment area, i.e. it is better to be born in Lancashire than, say, the West Country where football opportunities are fewer. The star names belong to players in the top First Division clubs, and these are footballers you automatically associate with their clubs and with international football. Yet there can be a danger in a large First Division club – with a squad of up to thirty first team players – of literally getting lost in the crowd.

At Arsenal, the names of Frank McLintock, goalkeeper Bob Wilson and fullback Bob McNab come to mind, but what of players like John Roberts or John Ritchie who are less often in the news. West Ham is well known for Bobby Moore (and until recently for his World Cup colleagues Martin Peters and Geoff Hurst); but what of Bonds, Ferguson or Tommy Taylor?

It is Manchester United, Manchester City, Leeds, Liverpool, Chelsea that breed the really big names of football: George Best, Bobby Charlton, Denis Law (United); Colin Bell, Francis Lee (City); Billy Bremner, Jack Charlton, Allan Clarke (Leeds); Kevin Keegan, Emlyn Hughes (Liverpool) and Osgood, Kember, Bonetti, Garland, Hudson, Webb (Chelsea).

This elite group of players are the ones who earn the top money, up to £10,000 a year, get written about and photographed on the sports pages and in football magazines. It is a select band, the membership of which constantly changes as players grow old and fade away (remember Greaves, Mackay, Hurst?), thrusting new youngsters like Arsenal's Charlie George or Derby's Colin Todd or Sheffield United's Tony Currie bid for places.

In spite of the concentration of stars in the top clubs – and we are talking about a group of twenty or thirty players out of nearly six hundred in the First Division – sometimes whole teams fail to attract the glamour of publicity that leads to top billing of their goal scorers. Examples are Coventry, Crystal Palace, to a certain extent Everton, Ipswich, Stoke, West Bromwich and Wolves. Clubs such as these are either overshadowed by large, more publicity oriented set-ups, or are situated in a football wilderness – such is the fate of Ipswich and Norwich. These clubs could also be regarded as 'unfashionable'; they are just out of the top league, do not win major prizes at home or in Europe, so the result is they do not attract the best players and their home-produced talent, if any, is usually sold off to more glamorous clubs.

Playing position will also affect a footballer's status. It is easier to get publicity if you are a high-scoring striker, and even if you are indolent and not a ball seeker, all will be forgiven as long as you keep scoring the goals. Examples of this type of player are Osgood of Chelsea and Clarke of Leeds, players that can exasperate for their apparent lack of effort, but are consistent high scorers, Osgood 85 for Chelsea and Clarke 47 for Leeds (up to end 1971–2).

Fullbacks are probably the least glamorous of players, though their status got a lift with the sale of Leicester's David Nish to Derby for a record quarter of a million pounds in 1972. Goalkeepers, because of their uniquely responsible the-buck-stops-here position, attract sympathy and glamour: just outside the action but there when needed. England goalkeeper Gordon Banks probably topped the list, followed by Chelsea's Peter Bonetti and Peter Shilton of Leicester. And Arsenal's Bob Wilson is known to thousands of mothers through advertising shoes on television. Up-and-coming goalkeepers include Ray Clemence of Liverpool (purchased from lowly Scunthorpe for a song), Derby's Colin Boulton, and two goalkeepers with the same name – Phil Parkes of Queens Park Rangers and his namesake at Wolves.

A footballer's ability, coupled with the right breaks, can increase his mobility and rather like the mobile executive in modern business he can move from club to club where his talents are most wanted and where he can command the right price. His mobility is not entirely unrestricted, as we have seen from the retain and transfer system that still operates in the League.

MOVEMENT OF PLAYERS

In an overall look at the ninety-two clubs, it is hard to find a general pattern of movement or stability, with the exception of

Sunderland's first team squad of twenty-nine, all but three of whom at the time of writing had only played for the one club. The three exceptions were two Scotsmen and Dave Watson, who was previously with Notts County and Rotherham.

Some players seem born to be mobile and the record is currently held by Tony Hateley (once voted player of the year in a private poll among footballers). Hateley has probably made around £20,000 collected in 5 per cents from moves that have taken him from Notts County to Aston Villa to Chelsea to Liverpool to Coventry to Birmingham and back to Notts County. Hateley is an average scorer of goals – one every two or three games – and must be given due credit for an ability to sell his talent to seven managers in a space of not many more years.

Trevor Hockey, a likeable player with a wild Nordic appearance, has the distinction of having played on every ground in the Football League, as he worked his way up through Bradford City, Nottingham Forest, Newcastle United and Birmingham City to Sheffield United and then Norwich, and Aston Villa, playing in all four Divisions.

A player of more than average talent will need to make one or two moves if he finds himself stuck at the 'wrong' club, and it will usually be the second or third that takes him to the top, though it can happen sooner.

A former colleague of Hockey's, Tony Currie, came to the front when he moved to Sheffield United from Watford. Colin Todd blossomed largely as a result of his move from Sunderland to Derby County. Leed's striker Allan Clarke did it on his fourth move – Walsall, Fulham, Leicester to Leeds. Keith Weller struggled unknown at Tottenham, then dropped a Division when he signed for Millwall, jumped from there to Chelsea (briefly) and then to Leicester. Roger Hoy started with Spurs, then joined Crystal Palace, moved from there to Luton, and then to his present club Cardiff City. Chelsea's Steve Kember made it in one move from Crystal Palace, as did his team mate Chris Garland from Bristol City. The two Manchester clubs are strong on home-grown players, though for some it is their second or third club: City goalkeeper Alec Stepney came via

Millwall and Chelsea, Ian Ure from Dundee and Arsenal, and Martin Buchan from Aberdeen and Ian Moore from Notts Forest. City is more of mixture, and for Colin Bell, Francis Lee and Mike Summerbee it is their third club; while Rodney Marsh joined them from Fulham and QPR and Wyn Davies from Wrexham, Bolton and Newcastle.

THE ONE-CLUB MAN

Some players, however, do not move around and for one reason or another are firmly one-club men. Such players include the famous: George Best, Bobby Charlton and Brian Kidd have always played for Manchester United, Gary Sprake, Billy Bremner, Jack Charlton, Norman Hunter, Eddie Gray and Peter Lorimer have played for no other club save Leeds United. Everton contains a high percentage of home-grown players, including Peter Scott, Tommy Wright, Colin Harvey and Joe Royle.

Crystal Palace's goalkeeper John Jackson is a one-club man, and together with David Payne are but two players among a host of Scottish imports. Ipswich and Norwich – clubs to which no one moves and from which no one leaves! – are largely made up of local talent, and the pattern is repeated in other First and Second Division clubs.

It is, surprisingly enough, when you get lower down the scale into the Third and Fourth Divisions that you get a number of clubs with mixed sides, and a large percentage of outside purchases, either from clubs in the same Division or older players from better clubs eking out their last years in football. Peterborough in the Fourth Division has hardly a single player who grew up with the club; most have moved in from clubs as diverse as Arsenal and Fulham. Not a single first-team player at Rochdale (Division Three) started originally with the club, yet eight out of seventeen players at Scunthorpe are local players.

It is a depressing thought that these less-well-off clubs, if they do develop their own talent, have to sell their best players and buy replacements, but mostly it is a case of maintaining as few players as possible, without reserves or apprentices, and buying hastily (and too dearly?) when injury forces the manager into the transfer market to seek a replacement.

Local loyalty is therefore hard to generate, when the team is made of imports from other clubs or even from outside the League (e.g. from Scotland or Ireland), and this makes for poor gates and further depresses football in the lower regions.

PLAYERS' WAGES

The life styles of the elite of First Division players, as portrayed and exaggerated by the popular press, can easily give the impression that all footballers are earning £100 a week, own boutiques or ladies' hairdressers, and drive fast and expensive cars. This, sadly, is not the case. Wages, as we have seen, have improved since the so-called new deal, following the strike by players and the judgment in the George Eastham case in the early 1960s – little over a *decade* ago.

Players are now to some extent freer to negotiate their own contracts and bargain for what they think they are worth. Pay is a topic that no player and few managers will discuss openly, and contracts and wages are jealously kept secrets.

However, the average top player should be able to secure a basic income of £5,000 to £6,000 a year, and up to £10,000 in exceptional circumstances. This sum can be increased by an elaborate system of bonuses, so much extra for a win, so much for a draw; progress in the League and FA cups; cash for points and appearance money. There may be quite substantial bonuses for reaching a certain level in the League table, and as much as £1,000 or more a man for winning the Division championship. Bonuses are still higher in competitions like the FA Cup, and if a team reaches the final then the players' pool comes into operation, with extra cash being earned from interviews and public appearances, dances, and a share of the newspaper and television coverage.

Top clubs will also be involved in European football and here the pickings are still richer. And players taking part in inter-nationals for England, Ireland, Scotland and Wales or Eire draw

a personal fee for appearing in these games of around £150 –
not bad for 90 minutes' work.

Lower down the Divisions, bonuses may be related to
attendance figures – a subtle ploy, as success on the field should
bring the crowds in. The payments are usually so much per
thousand spectators over a given minimum, say, 25,000 in the
First Division, higher for a successful club with regular gates
of 40–50,000.

The less successful clubs in Division One and run-of-the-mill
clubs in Division Two cannot afford to pay out such sums.
For this reason they cannot expect to attract and retain the
top stars though Crystal Palace reputedly pays high wages
to attract new signings. Wage rates are therefore likely to be
under £4,000 a year in the First Division, and still less,
under £3,000, in the Second. These rates are not high, about on
the level with a London docker or a Midlands car worker, and
one Second Division player complained to me that without
his 'appearance money' and bonuses, his flat weekly pay was
£30, from which came tax and National Instuance and the rent
(£4 a week) on his club-owned house: he was left with £22 in
his pocket, as much, as he pointed out, as he could be getting
digging holes in the road.

Compared with other branches of the entertainment industry,
football salaries are small, bearing in mind the comparatively
short playing life of a footballer, ten or fifteen years if he is
lucky. There *are* extremely young players making their mark in
First Division football, like Trevor Francis of Birmingham and
Willie Donachie of Manchester City. By comparison with
them, George Best and Rodney Marsh are old men, their
seniors by nearly ten years. But football at the top level takes
its toll in physical and mental wear and tear, and once he has
reached thirty a player is past his peak. There are exceptions of
course, like the Charlton brothers or George Eastham, but
around thirty most average players start the slow decline down
the Divisions or get out while still on top. Jimmy Greaves,
George Cohen, Dave Mackay did this. And Geoff Hurst was
at one stage thinking about it.

Some clubs pay bonuses for long service, to reward loyalty and discourage mobility. It is players with a long record of service at a top club like Arsenal or Manchester United who are probably the largest steady earners, though this system of long-service payments can upset younger players.

By contrast, the player who moves around can pick up useful bonuses, in the shape of 5 per cent of his transfer fee, provided he has not requested the move himself. David Nish's move from Leicester to Derby in August 1972 would have netted him some £11,500 in this way, enough to buy outright a modest house near his new club.

In the lower divisions, players are sometimes helped out by being found a club-owned house, which they rent for a nominal sum, often as low as £5 a week for a two-bedroomed semi in the Greater London area. Or they are helped with loans and mortgages.

Unfortunately it is not until he gets married that the player is allowed the privilege of living in his own home. Until the great day, he is obliged to live in approved digs, vetted by the club. Football's most famous bachelor George Best suffered this fate, until he persuaded the club to let him live in his newly built £40,000 show house: but when Best had another of his disappearing episodes, part of the punishment was a return to Mrs Fullaway's homely digs until team-mate Pat Crerand and his wife offered to put up the wayward winger in their own home.

COUNSELLING PLAYERS

It is not surprising therefore that young players tend to seek early marriage, at the very least as a means of escaping from the constraints of a watchful landlady. All the emphasis at the club, from the directors, manager and trainer, is on getting married and settling down. Almost everyone involved in the Best affair has counselled marriage as a way of solving his 'problems'. A player, however, may not want to marry, or supposing he is a homosexual? We have yet to see the day when United's centre forward sets up house with Rovers' goalkeeper, but it may come, and what will the amateur counsellers have to say about *that*?

Early marriage is not necessarily the stabilizer and cure-all that managers seek, although young players receive lectures on their private lives – as at Leeds – one may question the authority of those who take it upon themselves to give them. Certainly players *are* in need of guidance, but this should not necessarily come from within the club. Directors are usually successful local businessmen – builders, butchers and the like – and not qualified to advise youngsters about their morals or their sex lives. The manager is usually a busy, harassed man, concerned with success on the field and the security of his own job, and has a vested interest in seeing his players settled into early domesticity and a tied house: it discourages requests for a move if this would involve a major upheaval. The trainer, who spends most of his time with the younger players, is, we must admit, usually a man of limited experience and outlook, heavily pressured by those above him, a man who has invariably spent all his working life connected with football, maybe even at the same club.

Yet, incredibly, players tell me of the standard pre-marriage lecture given to them when they announced their intentions, which includes injunctions about the weakening effect of sex! 'Nothing after Wednesday if you're playing on Saturday', is the standard regulation, despite the findings of medical authorities such as Chesser and Reuben who have debunked this myth for several years. (Cf. *Sex and your Squash Life* by Dr Craig Clark.)

Footballers are not necessarily intellectuals or even very intelligent, nor need they be, but for this very reason they are peculiarly vulnerable to the good or bad advice handed out to them. The first team player leads a fairly cosseted existence, in which arrangements for his welfare, travel and hotel accommodation are taken care of by the 'office', so much so that one player asked me, at 24, how to go about booking an airline flight.

Coercing players into early marriage can lead to a number of serious breakdowns in the relationship. Players tend to marry the little girl who waited for them outside the dressing-room door, and there seems to be a predominance of hairdressers and shop assistants among football wives. Unfortunately, as a player progresses in football, his social horizons open up: he is fêted and sought after locally as a guest or after-dinner speaker and – as Francis Lee pointed out after his health breakdown – you can get caught up in a veritable whirl of social engagements.

Travelling away with the team, the player gets used to first-class rail travel and the best hotels. If his club competes in European competitions or he himself is an international, he gets the chance of travel abroad, and new sights and experiences. Numerous clubs arrange close-season tours overseas, so that by the time he is in his early twenties the player can have seen a lot of the world. Admittedly, not all of this may have actually rubbed off on him, and there is a tendency to see little more than the airport, the team coach and another stadium. But inevitably, something must get through.

Meanwhile, the little wife is left at home surrounded by the *material* benefits of her husband's success, her only company usually the wives of other players bemoaning the absence of their mates. They can only observe the changes occurring in their husbands, as they grow more confident, more worldly wise. Gradually a crack in their relationship will appear: the player has outgrown his wife, and another football marriage is heading for a breakdown.

This may seem like an exaggerated picture and I have met several charming wives of footballers. But if the player's mental development is neglected, as it most certainly is, what of that of the poor wives? Even at the top level, football is very much a part-time occupation, and lower down the Divisions a young footballer finds himself with a lot of time on his hands. Training takes up most weekday mornings only, and it is only in the early season that he will be playing more than one game a week. Once a fortnight he will travel to an away match, sometimes overnight if the distance is great, but he will be back for Saturday evening. Sunday is free and – if the team has done well – maybe Monday also.

There is an awful lot of time left to fill in, and when I have asked players about this, invariably they confess they hang around at home, doing odd jobs in the house, or driving over to pick the kids up from school or the wife from a visit to the hairdresser or a shopping expedition. Inevitably they feel 'they should be doing something about it', but the question is what, and to whom can they turn for guidance?

Some clubs interfere considerably in their players' free time, either actively encouraging or discouraging off-the-field interests. Curiously, they are usually clubs that are not very successful and they compensate for their own insecurity by meddling in the lives of their players. It is these clubs which place restrictions on talking to the press and which make players ask for permission before they can engage in business.

More successful clubs, notably Leeds, Manchester United and Manchester City, worry less about what their charges do off the field. It may be argued that there is not much they can do about it – if George Best decides to build himself a house and go and live in it. But usually it is because successful clubs have successful managers, men who have come to terms with themselves.

A NEW TYPE OF PLAYER?

Has the new deal attracted a new type of footballer? Superficially it might seem so. Hair is longer and shorts are shorter, and players tend to display some of the flashier trappings of their new-found wealth: smart cars, new clothes, trim houses. In spite of all this, however, footballers have not quite made it socially. They may wear their hired tails and toppers in the best traditions of the society wedding, but they are still tied to their class.

Most footballers, like the majority of sportsmen in the popular fields, come from working- or lower-middle-class backgrounds. This is probably because at comprehnsive and grammer schools more emphasis is placed on football than other sports. There is a sprinkling of GCEs among players and the occasional university graduate, like Steve Heighway of Liverpool, but it can be argued that a lack of brains is an advantage if you dedicate yourself to a life of physical training that takes up most of the working day. The intellectual could find such a regime irksome.

Pop stars are more likely to transcend the class barriers, but in a reverse direction. A good example is Mike d'Abo, a former Harrow schoolboy and son of a stockbroker, who has become typically classless and basically left wing in his outlook. Footballers on the contrary try to improve themselves, so that as *The Sunday Times* reported there is only one socialist among the Tottenham players. It is indeed ironical that footballers who fought for their rights through strike action just ten years ago and whose fathers are dockers and labourers abandon their working-class values as soon as they become even moderately wealthy.

One detects here again the influence of the small-town businessmen who cluster round almost any club. Directors are self-made local tycoons, not the sort to embrace socialism, and whose values are aggressive materialism. It is not surprising that players tend to adopt the same attitude, as they lack exposure to other influences.

What is even more deplorable is all lack of cultivation of the *mind*. It cannot be easy for a young man in his late teens and early twenties to cope with the problems that come with newly acquired wealth and regional or national acclaim. What is surprising is that more players do not do off the rails, and get wildly drunk or fly to London to go night-clubbing with some model or starlet. Maybe the disciplines of daily training and personal contact with team mates act as an anchor; we have yet to read of footballers turning to pot like contemporary pop stars to relieve their agonies or frustrations.

FUTURE OUTSIDE FOOTBALL

This lack of education will of course tell in later life, and many a player I asked about what he planned to do when he left football simply admitted he didn't know. Most would like to stay in the game, but there is only room for two or three hundred managers and coaches – 10 per cent or less of the number of footballers. The most popular activity outside playing football is coaching, and many players get jobs coaching at schools or evening institutes. This may prepare them for future positions as PE teachers, but once over 35 or so the opportunities will be fewer in what is essentially a younger man's profession.

Some players go into business, either with their wives or with friends they have met through football. The story goes that when Liverpool started the practice of travelling overnight to away games, even though these were fairly close by, a deputation of players went to manager Bill Shankly and protested at the arrangement: it cut into Friday afternoon's business at the boutique or betting shop.

England captain Bobby Moore has numerous business interests, including a factory producing leather clothing, and a share in a country club; and it is significant that when Geoff Hurst was debating his future in football, he met with his advisers at the West End offices of his sports clothing firm. Players set up a variety of enterprises. They include Don Rogers' sports shop in Swindon, a west London ladies' hairdresser's run by John Collins, captain of Cambridge United; a delicatessen run by David Court of Luton; a building firm run by Harry Cripps of Millwall; and Mike Channon of Southampton runs a men's hairdressers.

Some players try something more glamorous – Manchester United's Willie Morgan acts as disc jockey at a night club in the town; Dick Edwards of Torquay has formed a pop group; and Derek Dougan, chairman of the PFA, hosts chat shows on the local radio station.

One of the most famous businessmen footballers is Francis Lee of Manchester City, who runs a successful paper factory, but doyen of them all was George Best. Originally in the boutique business, he made his money from lending his name to sports products, foodstuffs, articles, books and annuals, probably earning some £30,000 to £40,000 a year outside football.

Not all players are so fortunate, and occasionally wrong advice or errors of judgment cause a business to fail. Because its owner is a prominent sports personality, such an event attracts inordinate publicity and managers and others who are anti-business shake their heads and mutter 'I told you so'. It is unfortunate again that in the area of business players can get a lot of bad advice. A colleague who visited Manchester reported to me that some well-known players 'were surrounded by the sort of spivs players were warned against when they were apprentices'.

Cashing in on one's name is not a new occupation for personalities: boxers Billy Walker and Terry Downes have done it successfully, through shrewd enterprise and good business management. Professional golfers and tennis players are handled by agents like Mark McCormack, in much the same way as showbiz entertainers leave the management of their careers to the Grade Organization or CMA.

Football agents started attracting attention in the late sixties, and within a year or two it was almost impossible to speak to a name player without the lad first consulting his agent. Perhaps the best-known agent and almost certainly the first in the field was Ken Stanley, a dour Yorkshire businessman who still runs his organization incongruously from an address in Huddersfield. Stanley's most famous client is George Best, and he also handled the affairs of the World Cup players' pool in 1970. Making money out of footballers is not as easy as it sounds, there being a limited supply of really international names. Stanley's success led to a crop of agents coming into the market, with some spectacular failures.

Before the World Cup there were reports that Stanley would make £200,000–£300,000 for the players' pool of thirty footballers, but the results did not come up to expectations. Footballers do *not* have the drawing power they think they have, and success on the field and the resulting limelight can end all too suddenly through accident or sudden decline of the team. Peter Marinello suffered this fate, appearing on posters advertising milk at about the same time as he was turning out for the Arsenal reserves.

Product endorsements by entertainers in other fields are common enough – Jilly Cooper uses a certain margarine, Andrew Cruickshank likes mature cheese – but apart from sports goods, men's toiletries and products that appeal to adolescents there is less scope with footballers. And I seriously wonder if the public are taken in by it all any more.

Veteran journalist Peter Wilson, appearing on the *Today* programme at the time of his retirement from the *Daily Mirror*, deplored the exploitation of footballers by businessmen. 'Unfortunately', Wilson commented, 'these lads just don't have the brains to sort out the good offers from the bad'.

What is at least as reprehensible is the lack of encouragement and opportunity to improve the footballer's standard of education. In his study of players from Tottenham Hotspur, Hunter Davies★ analysed the educational background and general interests of their first-team players. Only three had collected any GCE 'O' levels and in reply to the question did they follow current affairs, most were 'not interested' or, as Joe Kinnear puts it: 'Outside football, I don't know anything. The world could be coming to an end, and I wouldn't know unless it was on the sports pages'.

The footballers' choice of reading consisted mainly of the *Sun* and the *Daily Mirror*, with the *News of the World* and *The People* for weekends. Only Mike England admitted to taking *The Daily* and *Sunday Telegraph*, while Martin Peters stated flatly, 'I don't read books'.

Surprisingly, in spite of the generally low standard of intellect among players, you get the occasional football intellectual. Crystal Palace's Charlie Cooke has a reputation for deep thinking, while Rodney Marsh studies oil painting. Steve Heighway and Brian Hall of Liverpool are both graduates, along with Alan Gowling of Manchester United. But too few run-of-the-mill players are doing anything about further education: one of them is Peter Scott, an Everton fullback. Scott signed as an apprentice for the club against the wishes of the headmaster of his school, Ruffwood Comprehensive at Kirkby. He was a bright pupil and likely to get 'A' levels and the chance of a university place. The club however agreed to his taking a course at a technical college two days a week and he now studies by correspondence for his 'A' levels.

What is even more pernicious is the possibility of football poaching future players even from the universities. The manager of Swansea City admitted he had four students on his

★ Hunter Davies, *The Glory Game*.

books who, with training, could make his first team side within a year. 'But there's little chance of this. They've set their minds on getting degrees' he said, with what appeared to be a mixture of admiration and regret.

In the topsy-turvy world of the 1970s, when ladies' hair-dressers can earn as much as cabinet ministers, or fashion photographers as much as industrial tycoons, it is not surprising that professional football will become increasingly attractive as a means of earning a good living for more and more young men. And conversely, when possession of a university degree is no longer an automatic passport to an attractive secure job, school-boys throughout the country must be questioning what educa-tion is all about; nor is it surprising that parents are putting pressure on youngsters to leave school early and get some sort of job. What is wrong, however, is the cradle-snatching activities of certain clubs and the enormous amount of wastage among football apprentices. The lure of top-class football is a powerful magnet for a young man of average intelligence, but probably only one in fifty makes the grade. The rest have passed the best years of their lives from 15 to 20 in an environment where there is no encouragement or incentive to continue studying 'just in case things don't work out'. No kid is going to consider that he might not make it to the top.

This attitude is reflected even among established young players: football is possibly the most insecure profession, when injury can end a career overnight, a team can decline, or your playing talents may not fit into a newly designed side, so that at the end of your contract and option period you are offered a 'free'. Yet few if any players face up to the facts and do some-thing about buttressing themselves against the possibility of failing in football. And even the player who has managed to find himself a more or less secure position with a stable club is not consciously preparing himself for early retirement at 30 or 35: yet such a time comes as surely as day follows night.

In our discussion of the players' union we have seen that some efforts are being made in this direction, but clearly they are not enough. And the reader may ask why one should express so much concern over, say, footballers, when pop singers can have a similar meteoric rise and short period of high earnings followed by a rapid decline into obscurity. But somehow young men in these professions seem to know how to take care of themselves and their earnings more effectively, and because they have more bargaining power with record companies and talent agencies, they can usually negotiate the terms they want. Many of them also move into music composition, writing film scores or advertising jingles.

There are very few associated avenues open to a professional footballer, beyond staying in the game as a coach or trainer, and that is not a very lucrative job. A footballer is also very much part of a team and, except in rare cases, not really expected to have a mind of his own. One of the worst offenders in this area are Leeds United – their players wear identical hair-cuts and identical blank expressions, as though whatever individual spark they might have had has been effectively snuffed out. I once observed the team at London's Royal Garden Hotel after an evening match: they were shepherded into a private room to watch television and a portable bingo game was produced to occupy the intervening twenty minutes between the end of supper and the start of the programme.

This crushing of the player's identity is reflected in United's methods of training and the resulting style of play. There is little room for individual flair and the result is that they are a team that attempts everything but always comes off second best.

The Leeds management argue that their approach is designed to ease the players' lives and allow them to concentrate only on football. Certainly everything is done for them: Leeds United is an all-embracing cocoon from the boot room and private laundry to the identical named track suits hanging up in the first team dressing-room. But the public relations gimmick of having the players go through their training routine on the pitch before Saturday afternoon games reinforces the impression of well-trained performing animals being put through their paces.

At the same time as clubs insist on this type of overall subservience to their demands, players are still left on their own for a large part of the day, drifting into local cafés and fish-and-chip shops, or passing the afternoon at the billiard hall or betting shop. It is not surprising therefore that time hangs heavy on their hands, when their minds are left uncultivated and a lot of the counselling they get is no more than ill-informed theory.

Another northern club prides itself on its staff canteen, 'no one leaves here without a good hot meal inside him', the manager told me proudly. I sampled a meal at this club: it consisted of a mess of pre-heated indigestible stodge, over-loaded with calories and with little protein or vitamin content. Clearly no one knew what they were talking about when it came to providing a balanced, nutritious diet suitable for top-class athletes.

On top of the players' physical well-being little concern is shown for the need to attend to their mental and emotional development. The result is that a player is unreasonably elated or despondent according to his team's performance, so much so that players admit 'they give their wives hell' if the team happens to lose. Such an attitude may be worthy of an immature schoolboy, but, one might ask what would happen if every average executive after a bad or indifferent day at the office went home and did the same thing.

A lot was written during 1972 about stress among top foot-ballers but no one has paused to analyse just what kind of strain (if any) players are subject to and why they apparently cannot cope with it.

On the purely physical side, two interesting pieces of research are being carried out. One is a project being conducted at Everton by a team from the Liverpool Polytechnic, that in-cludes a three-year examination of the physical and mental demands on players, and an assessment of their proneness to injury and powers of recovery. The other is in the area of research into injuries of the hip: the sort of thing that affected Arsenal's Bob McNab, Alan Mullery (while he was with Spurs) and Derby's Roy McFarland. The condition was usually referred to as 'groin strain' but is now being diagnosed as weakening of a joint, the *symphisis pubis*, in the pelvic girdle, aggravated by hard physical exercise; the result being that when

Chapter 8

The Players:
Some Typical Characters

By the time one has interviewed a couple of hundred footballers in the course of sports reporting, one reaches the
conclusion that there is no such thing as a typical player. However, in this chapter, I propose to look at a number of players
who may be regarded as types – some famous, some not so
famous, some shy, some extrovert – to give some idea of the
mixture and variety that exist.

MARTIN PETERS

I first met Peters in 1968 and then again two years later shortly
after he had left West Ham and moved to Tottenham. He is a
shy but friendly young man, who has not changed a lot over the
years. His hair is not long and he is not a flashy dresser. Off
duty, he looks like a young executive from a large company, an
image that suits the dignified mock-Georgian house in Horn-
church that he occupies with his wife Kathy, a former tele-
phonist, and their two children.

Martin Peters will soon be thirty and he has played for just
two clubs: West Ham and Spurs. He has collected over fifty
full caps for England and took part in the World Cup in 1966 in
England and four years later in Mexico. For many years he
played as part of a trio of England footballers at West Ham,
alongside England captain Bobby Moore and Geoff Hurst (who
moved to Stoke in 1972).

Peters is typically classless in his accent and attitude, though he says he votes Conservative but is not really interested. Tory ladies often call to try and elicit his support for their tea parties and whist drives. His politics might shock his father, a Thames lighterman, and the neighbours from his native Plaistow. An all-round sportsman, Peters play golf and cricket, but confesses he never reads books. His social life is almost non-existent: a few drinks in the local during the week and the occasional Saturday night out with a few close non-footballing friends. Bobby Moore and his other West Ham team mates still come round occasionally, and the locals have got used to the idea of having a footballer for a neighbour. He drives a Jaguar and collected a white Cortina as part of the World Cup perks.

On the field Peters is workmanlike rather than spectacular. He is not a great goal scorer, but he covers a lot of ground and it is not until you make the effort to look for him that you realize the extent of his contribution to a game. The England team manager once called him 'ten years ahead of his time' and Peters says he never asked him what he meant by it.

At a time when players were being accused of disloyalty for not accepting international duty with alacrity, Peters is proud to play for England and says that like most players he would do it for nothing, just the honour. He had a hard time of it in Mexico in 1970 and found that the intense heat forced him to cut out a lot of his usual hard running. The press were none too kind to him but Peters feels he did all right, and came back and wrote a book about it all.

His request for a move seems to have taken West Ham by surprise. Apparently, unknown to Peters, another player had just been in to see the manager, Ron Greenwood, to ask for a move, so that Peters' request made it seem as though all the players were suddenly ganging up on him. Again Peters got a bad press, and was accused of being jealous of the success of Hurst and Moore. He dismisses these accusations as nonsense.

Peters says he is grateful to Greenwood for all he did. He was happy with his move to Spurs, where he says the club's outlook is broader.

In spite of a comparatively smooth and uneventful career, in which he admits he has had few disappointments, Peters says he remains a confirmed pessimist. If he is picked for an international match, the letter usually arrives on Tuesday of the week before. If for some reason it does not, he automatically assumes he has been dropped rather than that the post might be late!

He is still wary of pressmen and took refuge at his mother-in-law's house when he found his home beleaguered by journalists after the Tottenham move. He has virtually no interests outside football and as to his lack of social life he declares simply, 'There is a sort of fringe football and showbusiness crowd, to which I just don't belong'.

TREVOR HOCKEY

By contrast Trevor Hockey is the complete extrovert. Four or five years ago even, while he was playing for Birmingham City before moving to Sheffield, he was regarded as some kind of Midlands folk hero. His hair was long by the standards of the mid-sixties and he was one of the first players to start wearing his football shirt outside his shorts, a fashion that lads on village greens all over the country now copy.

I first saw him during a game at Milwall. He was not popular, with the crowd. He spent the full ninety minutes harrying the defence like a terrier dog with a pack of sheep. Four years later I watched him again playing for Sheffield United, newly promoted to the First Division. He was booed as he went into a tackle, booed when he took a throw-in, booed as he walked off the field at the end of the game. His hair had got even longer, and was tied back with a sweat band (another fashion he started). He was sporting a beard and that, coupled with his small stature, gave him the appearance of an Old Testament prophet. He covered miles of ground and found energy to spare to harangue and exhort his players to still greater effort.

What then of the young man who provokes so much emotion among spectators? Curiously, Hockey is a surprisingly dedicated and serious young professional. He was born near Keighley in the West Riding and started his football career with Bradford City. He then moved to Notts Forest and then Newcastle, staying there until they got promotion at the end of

I

the 1964–5 season. He joined Birmingham City in November 1965 and then moved to Sheffield United in January 1971. Two years later he joined Norwich City, and then moved to Aston Villa.

It was during his five years in Birmingham that Hockey became something of a cult figure. He was popular with the crowd and with the other players, cheerful and always willing to have a go. He took up the guitar and folk singing and made a record. Someone started a fan club for him and the City souvenir shop regularly ran out of pictures and badges. One year he personally signed over a thousand Christmas cards sent out to members.

All the while, Hockey was silently pleading to be taken seriously. He took the written and practical exams of the FA to become a fully qualified coach. His fellow players were incredulous, so he confesses he kept his mouth shut during team talks and hoped his performance on the day would speak for itself.

As well as playing on every football ground in the League and in every one of the four Divisions in his career, Hockey has tackled virtually every position on the field except that of goalkeeper. He started as a right winger but because he was so small and light at the time he found he got no mercy from the heavyweight fullbacks he encountered in Divisions Three and Four. So he changed to a defensive role when he moved to Newcastle and then Birmingham City tried him all over the place, including the reserves. At Sheffield he settled into a midfield role.

One of Hockey's virtues is a kind of old-fashioned honesty. In spite of his pop star image, he lives simply enough with his wife and two well behaved young daughters. He tries hard to become part of the community in which he lives by, for example, coaching at a local youth club. He is also desperately keen 'to improve himself'. He tried going two nights a week to technical college to study engineering but found it hard going and a pile of unfinished homework lying in the cupboard was a constant reminder to him that he had not 'taken his schooling seriously enough'.

Even his severest critics have to admire his grit and determination on the field and managers tolerate his wild image

because they know he gives a hundred per cent effort. He drives
his car like he plays his football – always thrusting forward,
trying out new openings, attempting new tactics. And if you
resist the temptation to pat him on the head like a woolly
sheepdog, you will find beneath all the hair a thoroughly sincere
and likeable young man.

GORDON WEST

Everton's Gordon West will inevitably go down in football
history as the reluctant goalkeeper, for he it was who early in
1970 wrote to Sir Alf Ramsey and asked not to be considered
for a place in the England squad destined for Mexico. This
action earned West an instant if ephemeral notoriety and a press
that surprised him for its bitterness.

Until the pre-Mexico incident, West had been enjoying a
successful if unspectacular career in football. He was born in
Barnsley, the middle son of a host of brothers and sisters, and
grew up with one ambition: not to join his father and brothers
down the pit. He played football at school, as a centre half, and
eventually became captain. He found himself made into a
goalkeeper by accident when one day a local colliery team were
short of someone for a match.

He joined the ground staff at Blackpool when he was sixteen.
This was another accident. A friend was offered a job there and
told he could 'bring a mate along'. So for £2·50 a week West
joined the Blackpool ground staff. He did not do much training
and the club were not pleased when they found they had
acquired a goalkeeper when they thought they were getting a
centre half. He moved to Everton when he was eighteen.

He quickly settled down, bringing his fiancée from Blackpool,
marrying and moving into a house on the outskirts of Liverpool.
West's wife is a classical pianist, and he himself spends a lot of
time working around the house or adding to his collection of
rare British stamps. They take their holidays abroad but West
recalls that the holiday which gave him greatest pleasure was a
fortnight in a hired boat on the Norfolk Broads.

He is philosophical about the Ramsey affair, genuinely
surprised at the amount of publicity he received and surprised

that he was variously labelled as 'unambitious' or 'conceited', and accused of 'picking a place for himself in the England squad' by one football manager/columnist. A number of players sympathized with West's attitude and 'admired his courage'. But he regards the whole affair as no more than a personal decision and as a reflection of his ability to sort out his own affairs as he goes along.

His goalkeeping ability is largely self-taught and he expects to remain at the top until he is nearly forty. He trains hard and rarely smokes and admits he has not eaten bread or potatoes for years in an attempt to keep his weight below fourteen stone.

Unlike a lot of players he does not see his future inside football. When he eventually retires he would like to buy a small farm and train horses and bring up his children in a country environment.

He is a consistent player, who rarely misses a first team appearance for Everton. He is occasionally barracked by the crowd, usually during local derbies with Liverpool. Off the field he is reluctant to discuss his game. He told me once of an incident in a pub.

'A stranger came up to me and started discussing last Saturday's game. So I asked him what *he* did for a living. It turned out he was a plumber. "Right", I said, "why don't we sit down and have a chat all about plumbing then?"'

RODNEY MARSH

In March 1972 Rodney Marsh moved from Queens Park Rangers to Manchester City. The fee was a record for the time – £200,000 – and at last it appeared that the idol of thousands of west Londoners was gaining the recognition he deserved. Until the move, Marsh had been one of those anomalies in the Football League: a brilliant player stuck with an average Second Division side, who did not get an England team place until his late twenties.

For many Londoners, Queens Park Rangers was synonymous with Rodney Marsh and his move cost the club gates some 10,000. But football clubs, like governments, tend to survive even after the departure of one of their stars and the following season QPR were back on form and started the new football year with an unbroken run of wins and draws.

Ever since Maureen Cleave produced a gushing piece about Marsh for the *Evening Standard* he became the darling of the fans and press, who tried to build him up into something he simply wasn't. Marsh is a striking figure, six feet tall, with fair hair and blue eyes, who has modelled clothes for the glossy magazines. On the football field, he was loved for his histrionics and his ability to score goals. Marsh basked in the limelight and was always ready with the sort of comment he knew would make good copy: 'Women only come to football to watch the men's legs', or 'The only book I read is *Pears Encyclopedia*.'

Marsh is in many ways a typical shrewd self-made Londoner. If he had not made his mark in football, he would have succeeded in one of the newer smart professions like fashion or photography. He was born in Stepney, son of a docker, and watched his first football from the terraces at Arsenal. He could have gone to a grammar school but turned it down when he found they played rugby and settled for the local technical college.

Even as a boy, he trained for football seven days a week and joined his first team, Fulham, when he was in his mid-teens. Then he knocked himself unconscious heading a goal and was out of football for a year. He was told he would never be able to go back again, having lost his sense of balance; he is still stone deaf in his left ear. But he came back and eventually joined QPR.

Like a lot of cockneys, he is shy and suspicious of strangers. He leads a quite domesticated life, with his wife Jean and their two children. Without being or attempting to become a football intellectual, he spends a lot of time reading, mostly history and 'general knowledge' and studying painting. He has an agent to handle his business activities, which consist mainly of product endorsements and designing sports equipment.

The move to Manchester City has I imagine been a salutary experience. He moved up a division and the settling-in period with his new club was far from smooth. He became a middleweight among giants, and in a Granada television interview some months later revealed that his fellow players had treated his arrival none too kindly, a situation that appears to have hurt Marsh deeply. He started the 1972–3 season well, justifying the confidence placed in him by manager Malcolm Allison, and soon had the Maine Road crowd chanting the familiar 'Rod-nee, Rod-nee'; they had finally adopted him as City's answer to United's George Best.

Marsh cost Rangers just £15,000 when he moved there from Fulham in March 1966. He saw them become Third Division champions and win the first League Cup Final at Wembley. With his move to Manchester City eight years later, he represents a good example of the player who might have been overlooked without the right kind of move.

FRANCIS BURNS

Moving from a soccer hotbed to a football backwater can be something of an unnerving experience, as ex-Manchester United player Francis Burns found when he went to Southampton in June 1972. A Scottish international, Burns suddenly found that the club he had served sinced he was fifteen had decided they could manage without him. He was informed over the telephone that terms had been agreed with the new club and he looked so shocked his wife assumed that a relative had died.

So swiftly Burns became yet another player to up sticks and move house and family to a strange town, to find somewhere to live, to find new friends. Living in the close-knit Manchester community, the glamour of being a United player brought unexpected perks – discounts on everything from furniture to a new car – and he managed to sell his house to a football fan keen to purchase a property in which a player had once lived.

Burns settled quickly enough among his new team mates. One of them came over to him in the bank and started chatting as though they were old friends, he recalls.

His main concern was not primarily with the money he would be getting at his new club, but whether Southampton would

ball is bound to dull the edges of his play and, now approaching his mid-twenties, unless he makes a move soon the years will race by and before long he will find himself turning out for his 'benefit' game.

Barrett is a likeable, easy going young man, who lives with his family in Mitcham. Lacking direction, it is not clear how his career will end or what he will do once he leaves football. He tries to enjoy life as it comes, only occasionally complaining, but short of a Fulham revolution he is stuck with the club for the rest of his days, truly one of football's casualties.

ALBERT MCCANN

Albert McCann is another victim of football circumstances. Playing for Portsmouth is his greatest disadvantage. It is not a glamour club and reporters of the football scene rarely attempt to forage as far as this south-coast outpost. In spite of his lengthy blonde hair and boyish good looks, McCann has been in professional football a long time – close on fifteen years. He was born in Maidenhead where he went to the local grammar school and collected five GCEs and played rugby and hockey. He preferred football and had to get his games with a local youth-club side.

His first professional club was Luton Town. He stayed two seasons under two different managers and then refused to re-sign after a dispute about wages: it was about the time the ceiling was lifted following action by the players' union. He got onto the transfer list and was bought by Coventry, one of a clutch of players who joined the club just before the arrival of Jimmy Hill as manager. Hill quickly put up a number of players for sale, including McCann, and when Portsmouth made a bid and offered the chance to play first team football, he returned south after only a few months at Coventry. He has been there ever since.

Because of low gates and consequent lack of money, Portsmouth are very much an economy club. They cannot afford a youth policy to nurse along promising young players and they buy only occasionally. Their purchases are usually mid-range players from nearby clubs, notably Plymouth, though they did spend £40,000 to buy Mike Trebilcock from Everton in 1968: four years later he was given a free transfer by the club. Recent purchases have been Norman Piper, a promising midfield player from Plymouth Argyle, and Arsenal's Peter Marinello.

Tackled about his situation, McCann argues that his attitude is realistic and points out that with a pleasant house and a car he has done as well as most young men of his age. Often, he argues, there is little a player can do to improve his personal position and his success is bound up with that of the club.

McCann has now started into that unnerving phase when he is in and out of the first team and he must be wondering how much longer he can survive in Second Division football. He has given his club good service – over three hundred appearances – and if he lies awake at night he must truly wonder if it has all been worth it and what, if anything, the future holds.

COLIN WALDRON

A success story from the Second Division is that of Colin Waldron. Waldron has in fact spent most of his playing career in the First but went down when Burnley were relegated along with Blackpool at the end of the 1970–1 season. He is still a youngish player but has packed a lot of football experience into a comparatively short career.

He grew up in Bury, Lancashire and as a boy got a trial with the local club, eventually signing apprentice forms with them. Within eighteen months he was playing in their reserves and up against tough defenders in the Central League. He sustained an injury and had to quit football for six months after a cartilage operation.

He eventually returned to the 'A' side and then started travelling as a reserve with the first team squad. He got his first taste of League football during the 1966–7 season. Bury were going through a bad time, with several changes of manager, and one morning when, through error, he had not turned up for a training session, he received a telegram suspending him for two weeks. Waldron reacted swiftly by putting in a transfer request.

While on holiday at the end of that season he heard two other clubs were interested in him – Liverpool and Chelsea. He had hurried meetings with Bill Shankly and Tommy Docherty respectively, and decided to go to Chelsea. Docherty gave him a first team place, but just as he was finding his feet alongside players who had been his schoolboy heroes, Docherty got the sack and Waldron found himself back in the reserves.

After a game against Leicester reserves, he found two clubs again interested in him – Burnley and Birmingham City. He chose Burnley and once more moved home to the north.

Burnley suffers from being a small town of some 80,000 people. The club has a forceful chairman in the shape of Bob Lord and team manager Jimmy Adamson is a shrewd buyer and seller of players. Former Burnley players are scattered throughout the League – Steve Kindon at Wolves, Ralph Coates at Tottenham, Willie Morgan at Manchester United, Andy Lochead at Aston Villa.

Waldron quickly settled down at the new club and has invested some of his football earnings in a restaurant, partnering Manchester City's Colin Bell. At Burnley he will certainly get noticed. At the end of the 1972–73 season Burnley eased their way back into the First Division thus significantly improving this young man's chances of recognition.

STAN TERNENT

One of Burnley's less spectacular sales was that of Stan Ternent to Carlisle in the middle of 1968. It was a move that did not rate headlines except perhaps in the *Cumberland Evening News and Star*. Being placed where it is, Carlisle does not get much attention even from the Manchester editions of the nationals.

Ternent was born in the village of Felling, near Newcastle-upon-Tyne, and was spotted by a Burnley scout while playing football for Northumberland Boys' Club. He took the train to Burnley for a trial game, scored two goals, and was asked to join the ground staff for a modest £8 a week plus £1·50 towards the cost of digs.

He stayed with the club for six years, never really making his mark in the first team, and moved to Carlisle just before the start of the 1968–9 season. It is a small club that carries the minimum number of professionals, usually fifteen or sixteen players, so that fitness and freedom from injury are important factors.

In Ternent they have a resilient player. He spent nearly a complete season playing with a chipped bone in his ankle before the X-ray showed up what was wrong when he finally complained of nagging pain. Even then he waited for the close season to get it fixed – so as not to lose his appearance money.

STUART BOAM

It was the then Mansfield manager, Tommy Eggleston, who first got me interested in Stuart Boam. He sang the praises of a tall fair-haired young halfback who had come up through the youth scheme and was now finding his feet in midfield. The youngster was Stuart Boam, a local boy from nearby Kirkby-in-Ashfield and a former Notts County supporter.

I had a couple of opportunities to watch him. Once against Orient, where he held the Mansfield defence together like a junior Dave Mackay or Billy Bremner. Then at Queens Park Rangers, in the second round of the League Cup, where Boam had the unenviable task of close-marking Rodney Marsh. He had a disastrous game and was sick in the dressing-room afterwards.

Boam started playing professional football part-time, while he completed an engineering apprenticeship, training three nights a week and turning out with the reserves on Saturdays. Mansfield were surviving in the Third Division, invariably ending up in fifth or sixth place, then unaccountably at the end of the 1971–2 season they sank to fourth from bottom and suffered the ignominy of relegation. By this time, Eggleston had moved to Everton as assistant manager and Boam's talents had been spotted by Middlesbrough. He quickly signed and found himself alongside former England man Nobby Stiles and Sheffield Wednesday's John Hickton.

I watched him again at the start of the 1971–2 season, again against Orient, newly promoted to the Second Division. He was agile and more mature, and still a young player his best performances are yet to come.

Chapter 9

The Managers

I suggested in an earlier chapter that if you were to draw up a sort of League table, some managers would inevitably come out on top. Either by sheer force of personality, by their skill in moulding a successful side, or simply by their staying power, an elite few managers do stay at the top.

The securest managers are those happily placed at the head of successful First Division clubs, clubs with a record of League championships, FA and League Cup wins, and victories in Europe to their credit. The most vociferous are not necessarily the most successful and even top managers have their ups and downs; in this way, they are closer to the footballers they manage and it is interesting to see how the most modern and successful men are closer than ever before to their players, in terms of age and experience.

In spite of all this, Manchester City's then manager, Malcolm Allison, for example started the 1972–3 season badly (so did Manchester United) and at the same time Derby's Brian Clough had a lot to say in the *Sunday Express* and was reported to be prevaricating over a new service contract offered by his directors that included a gagging clause to try and restrain his outbursts.

The insecurity of management is built into the job and several of the men I have talked to in the past five years have since moved on. Joe Mercer has left Manchester City for Coventry; Stan Cullis has quit Birmingham; Allan Brown has left Luton; and Dick Graham has resigned as manager of Colchester after a shareholders' meeting. Bristol Rovers's Bert Tann has died.

To take a typical sample of managers, as with players, is not easy but the following list is fairly representative. I have included Bert Head as I had the chance to observe him throughout a season at Crystal Palace, although he left the club in May 1973.

BERT HEAD

To think of Bert Head in a track suit is as crazy as picturing the Queen Mother in a pair of dungarees. A West Countryman, Crystal Palace's Bert Head was one of football's inveterate schemers, a shrewd buyer and seller of players, whose experience has stretched across clubs as widely differing as Bury, Swindon and Crystal Palace, whom he dragged into the First Division in 1968-9 and in spite of predictions from the experts managed to hold it there – albeit just above the relegation zone until 1973.

Before he came to Crystal Palace, Head was admired especially for his ability to create teams almost out of nothing, by developing a youth policy. In a tougher division, this is not always possible: results are wanted quicker and replacements have to be brought (and bought) in to prop up a struggling side either to clinch a promotion drive or avoid relegation.

'Nobody', Head told me, 'has a monopoly on youth. No single club can corner the market. I proved this at Swindon of all places, where we amassed some £400,000's worth of talent mainly drawn from an area in which people said they simply could not be found.'

Head moved to Swindon in 1957. He is not sure why he took up the challenge – he had been assistant manager at Bury – but thinks it may have been because it was a return to his own West Country. He started by sacking fourteen of the twenty-five players but found there was no money for replacements: even the ground's main stand had been closed by the insurance company, until essential repairs were done to it, which the club could not afford.

'It was absolutely impossible to raise even £2,000 or £3,000 to buy any sort of player,' Head recalls, 'as this would mean the whole season's profit gone in one deal.'

K

Head was the first manager to introduce ground staff boys at the club, and many of his players were 16 or 17 and playing in the League. They were picked as the result of two pre-season trial games.

'I lined up the possibles against the probables, and had a team of youngsters against a team of older players. To my amazement the kids won, 7-1. I didn't know whether to laugh or cry. I went home a troubled man and decided to sleep on it. I came to the conclusion that another practice game was needed.

'Before going out onto the field I warned the players they would be judged only on their merits as to whether they would be picked for the following week's game. Out they went and the kids won again, 6-2.

'The day came for our first home game. As I watched from the trainers' bench, a very large set of players ran onto the field – the opposition. By contrast my lads seemed to float out, they looked so young and fragile.'

The first five games were murder, the boys were thrashed. Gradually however they emerged and soon they were appearing on television as the wonder boys of the West. Gates rose from 6,000 to 20,000 and Swindon hauled themselves from the Third to the Second Division. Some of the Swindon youngsters are still household names in football: Don Rogers (now with Crystal Palace); Ernie Hunt, now with Coventry; Rod Thomas, a Welsh International; and Manchester City's Mike Summerbee.

Moving to Crystal Palace in April 1966 brought Head into contact with the harsh realities of Second and First Division football. Since joining the club he had to buy over forty players, many of them second-strings who have since left the club or got out of football. In 1967-8 he picked up Trevor Dawkins from West Ham and the much travelled Mark Lazarus from Queens Park Rangers. In 1968-9, the promotion year, he added Mel Blyth from Scunthorpe who has truly blossomed in the First Division, Colin Taylor from Walsall, John Loughlan and Tony Taylor from Morton and Roger Hoy from Spurs (now with Cardiff). This was followed the next season with the purchase of Roger Hynd, Gerry Queen, Alan Pinkney, Jim Scott and two Danish players from Scottish club Morton. In 1970–1, he moved into the bigger leagues, picking up Alan Birchenall and Bobby Tambling from Chelsea, Liverpool's Peter Wall, and four other players. Then in the first six weeks of the 1971–2 season, he bought Bobby Bell from Blackburn, Jon Craven from Blackpool, Bobby Kellard from Leicester, Sam Goodwin from Airdrie, and John Hughes and Willie Wallace from Celtic. Most of these deals were financed by the sale of Palace's one home grown star Steve Kember, who went to Chelsea for £150,000 in September 1972. There were also numerous other signings.

Head was backed all the way in his efforts to shore up the Palace team by outspoken chairman millionaire Arthur Wait, a lifelong Crystal Palace supporter. The way was not smooth and Head has described his survival balancing act as like 'a thousand and one nights in death row'.

Throughout it all, Head had retained a lot of his West Country calm, which concealed one of the alertest managerial brains in football. But there is still a touch of nostalgia when Head recalls the palmy, less troublesome days at Swindon. Among his favourite innovations were his 'safaris'.

'We used to take away up to fifty boys – youngsters, schoolboys, professionals, amateurs – to Weymouth, where we would camp for two or three weeks close to the beach. We had our own tents, a cook, a swimming pool. We used to train before breakfast and believe me, eggs and bacon have never smelled so good as after an early morning's PT.'

BERTIE MEE

Cast in a very different mould is dapper Bertie Mee of Arsenal. Arsenal are traditionally a rich and successful club, who – although they are not consistent winners – are respected as a solid, professional setup. Manager Mee suits them. He came into management from quite another profession – he is a qualified physiotherapist, and is known for his gentlemanly manner rather than his outbursts in the press or on television.

In spite of having to handle players of the calibre and temperament of Charlie George and Pat Rice, Mee feels that club differences should be settled privately rather than in the full glare of press publicity. 'I consider it my job both to protect and support my players', he told me. And it is an attitude he hopes to pass on to his staff.

'I hope that a little of my approach rubs off on the players and it is important that a mutual respect exists from this point of view. It is also important that my staff practice this philosophy and I in turn have an added responsibility to help them create the mature environment that allows this kind of attitude. Obviously I am older than the players and indeed the staff, and it is therefore important that I help both groups in every possible way.'

As a man who came into soccer management from outside the game, Mee is conscious of the general need for football administrators to have some kind of training in 'man management'. Staff meetings are held at 9.30 every morning, when points can be raised and thrashed out. Mee likes to feel he can take a broad view and tries to maintain a certain detachment from the job. 'You get caught between the tram lines, so to speak, too wrapped up in football, in the club. I try to take an interest in other things and so approach my work fresher – but I may be kidding myself here.'

Mee's spare time is taken up with gardening, and his wife and two children. He maintains a small circle of close friends outside football and Thurdsay he regards as his night off. 'We go out for a quiet meal and talk about other things.'

Mee is sensitive in particular on two questions. Given his gentlemanly approach to football, I questioned him about comments that players needed a certain hardness to succeed. I asked him how he reconciled this – Arsenal are, after all, not a soft club.

'This comes back to the competition of the modern game. Success is demanded by the fans, the directors, all of us – and I have to produce an adaptable set-up within which success can be achieved. Sometimes it is hard to reconcile principles that may be dear to me, but situations have to be coped with in this as in any other job', he replied.

The other point was on the question of apprentices, at a time when despite the recommendations of the Chester Committee some clubs seemed to regard them still as little more than ground staff boys.

'Let me make one point clear. The Arsenal apprentices are here to learn their job and you will not find them cleaning up the terraces and dressing-rooms. They are not training to be groundsmen but apprentice professional footballers and therefore five and a half days a week they are learning their profession. Fitness training, technique training, tactics, films, hygiene and diet are just some of the things they must work at and understand.'

BILL SHANKLY

Born at Glenbuck in Ayrshire, Bill Shankly was one of a family of ten children. His father was a professional runner and also the local tailor. His mother was the sister of two footballers and four of his brothers grew up in the professional game. At the age of seventeen, rather than stay down the pit, he went to Carlisle, at first on a month's trial, then stayed on for £4·50 a week as an apprentice.

He soon attracted the attention of larger clubs and within a season he had moved to Preston. With them he appeared in two FA Cup Finals and won his first cap for Scotland in 1938 against England. He then spent the war years in the RAF.

After the war, Bill Shankly turned to soccer management, returning to his old club Carlisle. Then he had spells at Grimsby, Workington and Huddersfield. He went to Liverpool on 1 December 1959. He was not given a contract and prefers to be judged by results. Although in his fifties, Shankly still trains with his players and preserves the air of a somewhat ascetic man. He drives himself hard and expects the same kind of dedication from his players. He is friendly and approachable and when I met him most of our conversation took place in the modest office he occupies under the main stand at Liverpool. In fourteen years, Shankly has seen changes. When he took over, the club produced an average Second Division side. At the end of the 1961–2 season he had them champions and they finished eighth in the First Division the following season. They won the First Division championship the following year and again in 1965–6. They have stayed in the top half dozen ever since. In spite of all this, Shankly is remarkably modest about his contribution to the club's success.

'To my mind', he told me, 'a manager is no more than a glorified coach. It is only in this country we call them team managers, whereas on the Continent they are known as coaches. And you don't have to be an FA qualified coach either. Coaching is something that is born inside a man. Here at Liverpool, all our training is based on exhaustion and recovery methods. But there is really nothing new in football. I am still applying a lot of the methods I learnt with Preston before the war! Half the secret is knowing your players, what they are capable of and what are their weaknesses. This is something I try and pass on to the players: there are no secrets of playing success. It is a matter of members of the team being able to work well together, knowing each other. I know my players better than they know themselves.

'I believe in treating players as adults, yet I know that some of them occasionally need a little more than coaxing to get them to do the things I want. So then I put on the pressure. Give me a player who trains hard, and the results will be reflected on Saturday afternoon. Enthusiasm is everything for me, plus a certain amount of teamwork.'

Shankly has always at least one eye open for a bargain and his current first team line-up represents a shrewd mixture of adventure and experience. Goalkeeper Ray Clemence, an England Under-23 cap, cost a mere £17,000 from Scunthorpe – the same club that let youngster Kevin Keegan slip away in 1971 for £35,000. Keegan is now one of the most exciting young players to watch in the First Division. Other shrewd acquisitions include Emlyn Hughes, John Toshack and Steve Heighway. Shankly's big money buys are not always successful and he surprised everyone when he splashed out £100,000 for an unknown youngster from Wolverhampton in the spindly shape of Alun Evans. Evans never really settled into the Liverpool side and like Marinello of Arsenal the move did him no good; he transfered to Aston Villa in 1972.

Shankly's 'outbursts' in the press are often little more than 'casual remarks I happened to make within earshot of reporters. If I make a couple of team changes', he claims, 'the papers scream "Shankly axes So-and-so." We have to change tactics to suit conditions. A manager must have thoughts about *each* game that has to be played and evolve a system to cope with it.

'Competition is a good thing, but often a manager's hands are tied: to stay at the top, the best clubs need to buy the best players from other top clubs, and they are simply not available. In the absence of suitable players you have to fall back on defensive methods and sometimes we play 4–4–2 or even 4–5–1 formations! This makes for very unattractive football.' At the end of 1972–3 Liverpool were again League champions and Shankly was voted manager of the year.

MALCOLM ALLISON

Malcolm Allison is one of the most popular of the modern track-suited managers: outspoken critic of the England team and very much at home with his players and in front of the television cameras, Allison is the supreme example of the new professional young manager of the 1970s. As far back as the earlier 1950s he was working on coaching techniques that were far in advance of their time and many of his theories on football have been published in his book*. In spite of his comparative youthfulness, he has had a lot of years in football.

He first became interested in the tactical side of football while stationed in Austria in the army. 'I saw a lot of continental

* Malcolm Allison, *Soccer for Thinkers* (Pelham Books, 1967).

football, and what I saw impressed me tremendously. The continentals were way ahead of British footballers in skill and approach to the game, and I realized then that unless we improved our *technique* we were in danger of becoming a second-rate footballing country', he explained.

On his return to England, Allison played for Charlton and then moved to West Ham, a veritable breeding ground for future football managers, that have included Noel Cantwell, Frank O'Farrell and Malcolm Musgrove. At West Ham Allison found 'our training methods were useless, and the players not very fit. So I went on a course to Lilleshall to see if I could find some new approach to the problem of fitness.' He says he returned disappointed, finding nothing that he could use as a professional . . . 'the course was mainly about teaching football to kids and amateurs'.

He returned at least with some kind of training schedule and a newly acquired ability to teach it. His first real coaching job came however with Bath City, in the Southern League. His first step was to give the players a pay rise and then order them to train five nights a week. When he finally left Bath for Plymouth, Allison found the standard of play was higher at Bath 'only because there we were organized, made to believe in ourselves and the players were convinced they were good.'

At Plymouth Allison's methods began to attract attention and one of the people who came down to watch his team play one Saturday was Manchester City's Joe Mercer. The pair had met while Allison was with West Ham and had discussed training methods. Mercer was impressed and invited Allison to join him at Manchester City. Mercer was very much one of football's elder statesmen and the partnership worked well. Then in 1972, Mercer moved out of the club to Coventry City and Allison took over completely, signing a new five year contract with the club in May, 1972.

Allison inherited a club of solid young professionals, moulded very much in his own image. They included England players Colin Bell, Francis Lee and Mike Summerbee and to these he added London hero Rodney Marsh. In spite of all this, Allison's team started off the 1972–3 season with a run of disasters, spending weeks at the bottom of the First Division table, along with their rivals Manchester United. The only consolation to Allison might have been that United did no better, in spite of a rash of spending by manager Frank O'Farrell to the tune of £600,000 in seven months, buying Martin Buchan from Aberdeen, Ian Moore from Notts Forest and Allison's own Wyn Davies; to these United added Bournemouth's prolific goal scorer Ted McDougall in September 1972. Allison's theories and belief in himself and his methods must have been sorely put to the test, as astonished fans and an enquiring press asked themselves, 'Why this curious decline?'

Malcolm Allison has always been a disciple of positive football, long before 'total football' became a catch phrase at the start of the 1972–3 season.

'The game has become so big in this country due to increased coverage on television, higher wages, higher transfer fees, that the pressures have increased for everybody. Managers are on the defensive, they tend to play safe. I don't know how they can go on week after week living on their nerves, winning 1–0 one week, then drawing 0–0 the next. It's a field day for the courageous player to find himself against a team that doesn't want to attack. But there's a lack of character, lack of depth in the game: and it is disappointing to me to see managers afraid to be positive.'

Allison felt however that maybe a breakthrough was near in attacking play – significant at a time when unattractive displays on the field, coupled with violence and simply too much football, were being blamed for the alarming drop in attendances that marked the start of the 1972–3 season.

'Most of the really good sides', he went on, 'are pushing up the pitch to take the play into the opposition's half of the field. Yet people laugh at us when we say we are going to defend in the other team's half, but this is in fact what we are trying to do'. Surprisingly at the end of the 1972–3 season Allison quit Manchester to take over Crystal Palace, only to see them sink into the Second Division within a few days of his appointment.

BRIAN CLOUGH

A manager who has found a place for himself among the top elite and whose name can be mentioned in the same breath as that of Allison, Bill Shankly and Don Revie is Brian Clough, manager of Derby County. Despite his diminutive stature, unruly hair and a distinctive accent that makes him football's most imitated character, Clough has been an uncompromising spokesman for total football and an unrelenting critic of England team manager Sir Alf Ramsey.

It is now some six years since he took over as manager of Derby County but what is not so widely known is that running the club is very much a partnership between himself and Peter Taylor, a former goalkeeper who met Clough when he was transferred from Coventry to Middlesbrough, where Clough had returned after completing his National Service. Still in his thirties, Clough has made his mark in football by taking an unspectacular Second Division club to the top of the First Division (1971–2) and for his shrewd buying of players.

His purchases have included some seemingly incredible bargain buys: including Roy McFarland from Tranmere for a mere £24,000; or the £20,000 he paid for John O'Hare from Sunderland; or £30,000 for Alan Hinton from Notts Forest. Nor by contrast is he afraid to spend big money: £170,000 to lure Colin Todd from Sunderland, £110,000 for Terry Hennessey and a record £220,000 for Leicester fullback David Nish.

Nor have his purchases included only established players – he is not averse to dipping into the Southern League and paid £15,000 for Roger Davies, an unknown goal scorer from Worcester City. His persistence in seeking out players he wants and incidents like the infamous Ian Moore affair have not made him popular with other managers and the football hierarchy. Moore was paraded by Clough one Saturday afternoon as 'our new signing' only to transfer to Manchester United two days later for £200,000!

Clough is tough, passionate, left wing: he offered to join a miners' picket line during the coal strike and was once offered a seat in Parliament. He is devoted to his family of three children and worries about the inroads into his private life: he claims he has to change his telephone number three or four times a year to secure some peace and quiet, and says he works a seven day week for nine months of the year.

When Noel Cantwell left Coventry City Clough was among the names mooted by the club as a possible successor: at the time he was questioning his own future, and even thought of giving up football.

'Having won the League championship, I had to ask myself where do we go from here. I talked to Peter Taylor, I talked to the players, I talked to anyone. It just seemed the end of the road, time to get out. We felt we could always go back to Hartlepool and get a job.'

At the same time Clough was having problems with his own directors, anxious to curb his outbursts in the press and on television, and Clough was demurring about clauses in his new contract that restricted his freedom of speech. He felt he had a right to say what he liked to whom he liked, and he is no fool and recognizes that he is 'good copy'. 'Better one headline than a thousand words of copy', he argues.

Clough's personal detachment is something not often found in football managers and given his head he should over the years help to bring a little sanity into the game. Well liked and respected by his players, even his sternest critics cannot argue that his methods have not brought success.

DON REVIE

Don Revie is the manager Brian Clough would like to be like. Revie was, like Clough, born in a working-class home in the north-east (Middlesbrough) and remembers his father being out of work when he was a child. He did not possess a pair of football boots until he was eleven, and used to play in his wellingtons or an old pair of shoes with cardboard in the soles. He went to Leicester City as a boy of fourteen. In 1949 he transferred to Hull for a fee of £20,000 and two years later moved to Manchester City in an exchange deal. Five years later he moved to Sunderland.

When he took over the running of Leeds United just over a decade ago they were an average club in the Second Division – a Division that included many now more illustrious names such as Liverpool, Chelsea and Sunderland. Revie says he always wanted to go into management and when the chance came one of the first things he did was go and ask someone for advice about the job.

'Who better than Matt Busby', he recalls, 'because coming from the playing side I realized I knew nothing at all about management: travel arrangements, training schedules, how to handle players, how to deal with the press and so on. I spent two and a half hours with Matt and I think the most important thing he taught me was to make my own decisions and stand by them.'

Another piece of Busby's advice was to get a good staff around him, and this Revie did in the shape of Les Cocker, his coach, and trainer Syd Owen. The methods paid off, but for years Leeds became known as a ruthless and even dirty team, an image which Revie feels they are only just beginning to shake off. They got promotion from the Second Division at the end of 1963–4 and almost immediately shot to the head of the First – runners up the following two seasons and champions by 1968–9. Twice defeated in the FA Cup Final at Wembley, they finally won in 1971–2. They have been impressive in Europe also – picking up the European Cup, the Fairs Cup and the UEFA Cup on the way.

'I think being a footballer is like being a hungry fighter. You get right to the top and then there's nothing else to go for. This is why I have a tremendous respect for Liverpool. They have been very successful yet they still go out and look for fresh successes. They have this great drive – and that is something I try and impress onto my players.'

In common with most top managers, Revie suffers from the pressures of being at the top. He used to smoke cigars during a match, and when he found he got through twenty in an hour and a half, he decided to give them up. He now chews gum instead.

As the season gathers momentum Revie finds 'each morning I drive to the club a bit quicker, or I do everything just a fraction faster. Then suddenly the tiniest things start to irritate you.'

His wife Elsie says: 'It's the remoteness at home that gives him away. Sometimes he's not really with you and I think I could be talking to the wall for all the effect it's having on him.'

Revie's son Duncan has been educated at a public school and is now at university. He also has a teenage daughter. I asked him if he would let a son become a professional footballer.

'If he was really good, yes, but I would hesitate after seeing so many youngsters come here at fifteen and then two years later I have to call them into the office and tell them "Son, you've got to look for another profession."

'Seeing the disappointment on their faces is one of the toughest sides to being a manager: that's when the job really hurts you. I think if you have a good education you carry it with you all your life. I didn't get one, so I am glad my son is being more fortunate.'

TOMMY DOCHERTY

For sheer opportunist survival in football management the prize must surely go to Tommy Docherty, who took over as manager of Manchester United in December 1972, following the George Best/Frank O'Farrell débâcle.

Like being an ex-MP, there is no worse job than being an ex-football manager and men of Docherty's undoubted calibre rarely stay out of the limelight for long. Surprisingly his League experience is limited. He became coach at Chelsea in February 1961, following a playing career with Celtic, Preston and Arsenal. A year later he became manager, steering them back to the First Division. He stayed until October 1967, resigning after differences during an overseas tour and a month later joined Rotherham. By the following May, Rotherham had sunk to the Third Division and Docherty moved to Queens Park Rangers.

His stay with the west London club was brief, even by Docherty's standards – a mere twenty-nine days. That did not prevent his being snapped up again almost immediately, and this time he took off to revitalize Aston Villa. He left Villa in January 1970. The following month found him managing Oporto, Portugal.

Docherty left in April 1971 and the following July joined Terry Neill in an unlikely partnership at Hull City. Relief was however swiftly at hand, as by September he was offered the role of caretaker manager of the Scottish national side, following the departure of Bobby Brown. He became full manager eight weeks later. Thirteen months afterwards, Manchester United asked for permission from the Scottish FA to contact Docherty and after four days of speculation he took over the hottest seat in football.

Docherty is philosophical about his moves. 'Look', he told me, 'in this game you don't sit around waiting for jobs to come along. People soon forget you and you're out of a job. The Rotherham post came along and I was glad to take it. Then Queens Park Rangers gave me a chance to better myself. I parted from them after arguing about £35,000 I wanted for a player.'

What qualities Docherty brings to management are hard to define exactly. I observed his first few days at Aston Villa: the air was positively electric with activity. No one walked any more: they ran. And it is just this kind of enthusiasm that he brought to Manchester United.

Here too for the first time since Chelsea he had the players to work with, for in spite of their dismal performances United were not without talent. Nor should one overlook his work with the Scottish national side: it is thanks to him that Scotland looked like serious contenders for the 1974 World Cup.

At United, Docherty became probably the highest paid manager in the game, at a reported £16,000 a year, plus an elaborate system of bonuses linked to success. As Jeff Powell put it in the *Daily Mail*: 'Docherty may just turn United and the football world upside down. At the very least, it will be fun finding out.'

These then are just some of the managers. They represent a small percentage of the total, and many soldier on even inside First Division clubs rarely rating a headline from week to week except in their local papers. Once in management it is hard to imagine oneself in any other kind of job. As Vic Buckingham remarked on leaving Fulham: 'You simply have nothing to do on Saturdays.'

But like politicians managers have a habit of coming back. They are rarely out of work for long and although they may disappear for a season or two to look after some obscure continental side, they invariably return in a blaze of publicity to replace a sacked colleague or take over a struggling Second or Third Division club.

All managers talk of the pressures of football – pressures to stay successful if you are at the top, pressures to survive if you are near the bottom. None of them admits to having a secret formula for success and even skill and flair of the calibre of Malcolm Allison or Brian Clough cannot always produce results on the field.

Some managers have engineered themselves long and lucrative contracts and Leeds's Don Revie is deservedly probably the securest manager in football. Good managers are hard to find and retain and publicity conscious Coventry were reportedly offering up to £20,000 a year for the right man after the departure of Noel Cantwell in 1972.

It may take more than money however to lure the right man: good management is a combination of luck, resources, skilful buying and selling, and success. In football nothing succeeds like the last ingredient.

Chapter 10

The Spectators

'It is becoming dangerous for ordinary people to walk about Nottingham after football matches', a court chairman said yesterday.

'Magistrate Mr Brian Morley added: "This is something we are not going to tolerate. It is getting to the stage when people dare not go to matches. We have got a job in this court to protect the citizen from hooliganism." ' (*Daily Mail*, 26 September 1972).

The above extract was a routine report, following another weekend of 'violence' on the football terraces. It concerned the match between Second Division Aston Villa and Nottingham Forest (at Nottingham), where out of a crowd of just 14,000, police made 46 arrests and used mounted patrols and dogs to wade into the sparse crowd. It was a weekend too when 56 players were booked by referees and attendances at League games fell by an alarming 72,000.

Fines of up to £100 were imposed by the Nottingham magistrates, who added 'If we had the authority to do so, we would send you down.' Weapons confiscated from among those attending the game included an eight inch long gate spring, a ratchet operated Japanese knife, and a quantity of steel combs, screwdrivers and knuckle-dusters.

If you do not go to football matches, you could easily get the impression that every Saturday afternoon game resembles the storming of the Bastile or the Paris riots of 1968. I have been to hundreds of games and it is simply not true. Wide publicity in the press and on television is bound to give an exaggerated picture of the situation. Indeed on the Saturday afternoon in question, commentator Huw Johns devoted 90 per cent of his match round-up at 5 p.m. to what had happened on the terraces, not what had taken place on the field. Regrettable as violence is, it is purely a symptom of our times and the whole question is one that is in danger of getting out of proportion.

A lot of soccer writers and commentators get emotional about the so-called football fan. This conjures up the picture of the dedicated team supporter, done up in striped scarf and woolly hat, and waving a rattle. This image is about ten years out of date.

We have already found in another chapter that greater overall affluence, the earning power of the young, and the resultant greater mobility has produced a new type of football spectator: someone who can take his choice of the games he will go and see out of a variety of entertainment on offer any Saturday afternoon. London has a choice of a dozen clubs, and the same is true in parts of Lancashire and the Midlands. You can either choose the best First Division soccer or opt for a quiet backwater in the Second or lower Divisions.

Apart from isolated centres and the odd ten or a dozen clubs with huge working-class followings, the day of the dedicated fan has passed. In spite of this, football magazines are still apt to glamorize the dedicated supporter – running competitions and stories about men who get up at the crack of dawn to travel by coach or train or car to one of their team's away fixtures. You would gather from this that there is a mass movement of football supporters invading strange towns week after week, but this is simply not so.

The numbers of people who do travel to away games are surprisingly small and it is often all a hardworking supporters club secretary can do to get up a coach load or two of even the most dedicated followers to travel to a distant away game. True, a Wembley Cup Final will bring hordes of football fans into London, often the night before, and being gregarious by nature they tend to flock to centres of 'night life' like Piccadilly Circus or Trafalgar Square. This might give the impression that there is a mass movement afoot, but out of a typical 100,000 Wembley crowd probably less than a third are regular football attenders, due to the peculiar system of ticket distribution by the authorities.

But given that supporters do move from town to town, as often as not they are deposited by coach or train early in the morning before the game, with five or six hours to kill before the kick-off. With little money in their pockets, other than the price of a meal and a few drinks, there is little left for them to do other than roam in groups among the bewildered Saturday morning shoppers, before making en masse for the football ground.

RESPONSIBILITY OF CLUBS

Once there, to secure any kind of vantage point in the cheaper enclosures or terracing, you have to arrive anything up to two hours before the game. During the ensuing 120 minutes, more and more spectators are packed in behind and little is done to keep the attention and interest. For the last few minutes before the game, the club's public address system will blare out pop music, interspersed with 'requests' and announcements by an unprofessional disc jockey. This provides no more than background distraction which after a while can be ignored.

By this stage it is all but impossible to vacate one's vantage point to go to the toilet or find a cup of tea, and it is not uncommon for fathers to have to make their youngsters urinate onto the terracing through a rolled newspaper. It is not surprising that even before the game starts, tempers are frayed: thanks to an uncomfortable train or coach journey, often overnight; harassment by the police on arrival at the railway station and outside the ground; inadequacy of cheap eating places and overcrowded pubs, where the only nourishment is the ubiquitous pork pie.

And once inside the ground, little is done to relieve the supporters' discomfort. Toilet facilities are dirty and inadequate and it is often impossible to get anything to eat or drink. Some smarter clubs like Arsenal or West Ham occasionally put on a military band display and this does something to relieve the boredom, and Leeds United have tried putting their players circus-like through their training routine in view of the spectators. Other gimmicks have been tried, from fashion shows to parading the shiny new car that can be won in a raffle.

By denying them decent facilities clubs undeniably contribute to the misbehaviour of supporters. Unless you can afford to watch football from the covered seating, and often even then if the weather is inclement, it is necessary to get yourself up in some kind of outfit more relevant to a Himalayan expedition than a visit to a twentieth-century sports stadium. Many grounds still have turf banking behind the goal areas, which on wet days turns to a quagmire of slush. You don't wear your best shoes for this kind of outing, and a youngster's choice of his working boots is likely to be no more than a sensible precaution against the kind of conditions he will encounter once inside the ground.

I once met a young fan outside the Queens Park Rangers ground, the son of my local newsagent. He had been refused admission because he was wearing heavy boots and had the then fashionable cropped haircut. I took him into the stand with me on a spare ticket and encountered no complications on the way. He was typical of the thousands of ordinary working boys who may find themselves discriminated against by police and club officials simply because of the way they dress.

Some clubs are making improvements to cover larger sections of their grounds, but as car parking facilities are non-existent in most cases, it is still necessary to park one's car several streets away from the ground or walk half a mile or more from public transport, and in the rain this is not fun. Football grounds are not the enclosure at Ascot, nor would anyone want them that way, but on the other hand the facilities should not be so bad that spectators in any but the smartest seats are compelled to turn out in their gardening clothes.

FOOTBALL VIOLENCE

The very design of most grounds makes it easy for the small

hooligan element to make its presence felt. I am referring now not to bad facilities at the cheaper prices, which are almost universal, but the lack of effective means of segregation of the larger crowds into manageable groups. It is possible at many grounds for youngsters to position themselves behind one goalmouth and then at half-time walk the entire length of the side enclosure to reach the opposite end of the pitch: on the way they encounter groups of rival supporters doing the move in reverse.

There are bound to be clashes in a situation like this, but no more so than trying to make one's way out of a London Underground station at 5 p.m., when everyone is hell bent on pushing you back in the opposite direction. Allowing young spectators to roam the whole length of the ground is simply asking for trouble and the wonder is that more clashes do not occur.

I am not questioning any spectator's right to secure himself a good vantage point from which to watch the game. In the case of some grounds like Arsenal or Chelsea, if you arrive late you are lucky to see anything at all from behind a mass of bobbing heads.

Some grounds have, it is true, set limits on their capacity either voluntarily (as at Chelsea during their rebuilding programme), or through pressure from the police. But invariably communications between turnstiles are bad and often a harassed secretary is heard telling the press that 'the north bank turnstile did not stop admitting spectators until twenty minutes after I gave the order'. As a result thousands more spectators are poured into already overcrowded areas, and marshals armed with portable loud hailers have to ask those in front to move forward so that late arrivals can at least get off the approach steps and gain a foothold on the terracing.

Such conditions are dangerous given even the most well behaved crowds: if there is an accident or case of fainting, it is almost impossible to get to the victim quickly. And a sudden surge of movement following a goal or to get a better view of a touchline incident can carry you off your feet, arms pinned to your sides, until you find yourself cut off from your friends and deposited several yards from your original spot.

The wonder is that more violence does not occur, not that there is so much. Football is not like cricket or lawn tennis, and the bulk of the people who go to matches are young men who work in tough outdoor jobs and are not used to the finer points of discussion with their fellows. There is a lot of fairly good-natured baiting of players and the referee – a harmless enough sort of release. We have all heard remarks like 'Is that all you can do for £100 a week' hurled at the expensive forward who has muffed a pass or 'Send 'im off' when the opposition fullback brings down a home player making for goal.

Strangely enough, some of the most vociferous spectators are small men, quite mild in appearance and they often occupy some of the best seats or are holders of season tickets. Being a regular supporter gives some kind of licence to criticize, and there is little or no danger of retaliation from the objects of one's abuse. Rather like the ladies who sit and shout in the front rows at wrestling matches, spectators can hurl at players the sort of remarks they would like but are afraid to hand out to the foreman, the schoolteacher or even the wife. For often it is the mild, henpecked little man at home who becomes the loud mouth at a football game.

The influence of televised football in this context is interesting for thanks to the analysis of experts like Jimmy Hill and Brian Moore, with slow motion shots and action replays, there must be a greater awareness of the finer points of football. Everyone likes to think of himself as a football expert, and I am not referring to the sort of person who keeps up a running commentary during the game, assessing every move on the way. But skills are appreciated and even good efforts by the opposing forwards or a fine goal save by the opposition keeper will get sound applause from the crowd.

Involving spectators in the game is one of the keys to solving violence at matches. This can be done in a general way by raising the standard of football entertainment: at an exciting game, with plenty of action, skill and goals, you are absorbed by what is happening on the field, the time passes quickly, and you leave the game with the satisfaction of having spent a pleasant afternoon.

PLAYERS' RESPONSIBILITY?

There are arguments that violence on the field leads to violence among spectators, but personally I have reservations about this. In the seventies, there is much more violence around: vandalism that results in telephone kiosks being smashed or shop windows broken; armed robberies and raids on banks and wages offices; the advent of the muggers on Underground trains. This is the criminal violence.

There is also the violence of protest: we have been watching nightly reports of events in Northern Ireland for four years now. We have squatters fighting evictions, housewives protesting about motorways or pedestrian crossings, strikes and violent picketing, sit-ins by students, sit-ins by parents, rallies, marches, demonstrations. When one considers the behaviour of the dockers outside Transport House or at the container terminals, it is not surprising that youngsters who grow up in such an atmosphere of violence, whatever the rights and wrongs of the cause, prefer to use their boots and their fists rather than their brains to settle a dispute.

To lay the blame therefore on the players is unjust. We have seen already that modern players are subject to considerable pressures, as football has become a highly paid competitive business. As players get younger, they leave school earlier, and it does not follow that because they earn high wages they are necessarily better equipped mentally to deal with a flare-up on the pitch. A team that is under pressure, following a run of lost games or trying to escape the bogey of relegation, will be bad tempered and edgy on the field. A lot happens in the heat of the moment that is forgotten afterwards, and hands are shaken all round.

This does not excuse the type of player known to be 'a bit of a hard case' and who, as Jackie Charlton once pointed out in a series of astonishing revelations to the press, appears in a footballer's mental black book. This sort of conduct and talk is inexcusable and any manager should seriously take in hand a player who offends in this way, as it is this sort of violence that sickens even the most ardent supporters and turns them away.

NEW MEASURES

Following the Lang Report of December 1969, some clubs have taken steps to improve security on their grounds. Two clubs notably, Leeds and Derby, have responded by including a fully equipped police room built into the grounds, complete with detention rooms and two-way radio equipment. And in September 1972, reporters were surprised to learn that one Liverpool ground had a room complete with manacles, for restraining offenders.

Heavier fines and increased prison offences may have a deterrent effect, and certainly attract wide press publicity. Yet to the young, they must represent yet another example of the Establishment trying to repress their natural exuberance. Football offenders are, it has to be admitted, usually on the young side. In spite of the dire warnings of magistrates that no decent citizen will want to watch a football match, I have attended hundreds of games and witnessed little more than a few young boys of no more than twelve or fourteen being led out sheepishly by the ear by some red faced massive constable. In most grounds, that is the full extent of the 'violence'.

Another common 'offence' is that of the hordes of youngsters, usually even smaller than the terrace tearaways, who race onto the pitch at the end of the game. Personally I can see little harm in this. They are usually *very* young – ten, eleven or twelve years old, often much younger – and they want little more than to clap their favourite players, even the opposition, on the back and then race back to the safety of the enclosure before some large policeman moves in to carry them off. When Crystal Palace got promotion to the First Division, I witnessed a spontaneous mass charge onto the pitch following their game that clinched it. There were probably 20,000 spectators on the field, and the players responded by climbing up into the directors' box and taking off their shirts and throwing them into the crowd. Strangely no one complained about this invasion of the sacred turf.

Deterrent methods have only a limited effect: more success can be achieved by good public relations. I saw this in operation in a very personal way when ex-Crystal Palace manager Bert Head used to be surrounded on the train returning from away games by some of the so-called worst tearaways among the club's younger supporters. Head realized that while he and the team party were enjoying first-class rail travel and a hot meal these kids had paid hard-earned wages to travel on the same train, often without sleep and food, just for the glory of being close to their team.

Carried to a finer degree, the establishment and encouragement of supporters' social clubs is another step towards involving spectators in the affairs of the club. This was done with extreme success at Coventry under Jimmy Hill and clearly pays dividends, not only in terms of extra cash that can come into the club, but as an investment in public relations of the best kind.

Club programmes can also be used to develop a sense of belonging, becoming more like company house magazines than team sheets. This was attempted at Crystal Palace with the introduction of personal biographies of the players and junior staff.

Finally, if there has to be a long wait before the start of a game, is it not possible to stage junior or apprentice matches at, say, 1.15 p.m., so that early arrivals could watch at least part of the game? Or five a side competitions? Groundsmen may groan in horror at the thought, but pitches are grossly underused as it is, being occupied sometimes only once every fourteen days during the season. Such junior games would foster interest in the club's youth policy and at very least provide a distraction for the early arrivals and, one hopes, keep their minds off more violent actions.

Chapter 11

Running the National Side

The job of running a national side is rather like being a League team manager, except that you have an almost endless supply of top-class professionals to choose from. And apart from European games and home internationals, the manager of the national side has only got to prove himself every four years, at the time of the World Cup. When he joined Manchester United as manager in December 1972, Tommy Docherty said he had enjoyed running the Scottish team, but he got bored: there was simply nothing to do between fixtures.

England's team manager is Sir Alf Ramsey, who took over the job from Walter Winterbottom in 1962. Since then there have been two World Cups: Ramsey has won one (England beat Germany 4-2 after extra time at Wembley in 1966) and lost one (England lost to West Germany by 2-3 at the quarter finals in Leon on 14 June 1970). All the signs are that he will still be around for the 1974 World Cup to be staged in Munich, home of the ill-fated 1972 Olympics.

As Docherty brought enthusiasm and flair to the Scottish game, so Ramsey likewise has left his mark on the performance of England, often a dull pedestrian exercise, that has left football writers and supporters clamouring for more flair, more artistry.

Ramsey's own career as a player was largely uneventful. He was born in Dagenham and worked in a grocer's shop before joining Southampton. He then moved to Tottenham, and played for England as right back. He went into managment with Ipswich Town, an undistinguished club then lying in the middle of the Second Division. He made them Division Two champions and then pushed them to the top of the First.

It was when Ramsey took over in 1962 that for the first time the collection of possible and probable England players came to be regarded as a national 'squad'. The 1966 World Cup played during a glorious summer brought Ramsey even more firmly into the limelight and he gradually established himself as a mixture of father figure and diplomat. This aura of grandness was further emphasized when millions of viewers of television watched Ramsey lumbering across the Wembley turf to talk to the England players, when after ninety minutes both teams had reached stalemate. For the first time we could observe this avuncular figure in action, dignified and unruffled.

It is this image that consciously or not Ramsey has preserved. He is short haired and well groomed. He tends not to say much, which is frustrating for sports journalists with columns to fill, and when he does speak his utterances are invariably non-committal. He rarely discusses individual players.

Ramsey's detachment from day to day football – the fate of all national managers as Docherty pointed out – is bound to create a certain isolation and his aloofness has come in for a certain amount of criticism in the press and from other, usually younger, football managers.

There certainly appears to be something of a generation gap with the result that Ramsey tends to stick by old and trusted players from five or more years previously, until mounting criticism apparently forces him to introduce some fresh faces into the team. This cautious experimentation usually takes place during unimportant games. A typical example was his use of Currie and Channon in England's friendly game against Russia in June 1973, when clearly these players should have been used days previously, when England lost to Poland in a World Cup qualifier.

Trying out new players is a fine idea, provided one can detect a certain consistency of choice, and it is inexplicable that for all Ramsey's talent-searching forays into the First and Second Divisions a player of the calibre of Rodney Marsh was overlooked for so long. Ramsey's attitude reminds one of the BBC's towards new performers, 'We can't use you because we don't know you, but once we do you're in for life'!

It is unlikely that Ramsey will ever develop that distinct relationship between player and manager that exists, say, between Don Revie and Leeds United, Clough and Derby County, Malcolm Allison and Manchester City, or between Dave Sexton and Chelsea. Obviously relationships cannot flourish without the day to day contact in the dressing-room and on the training ground, though the England squad tends to get together more often and for longer periods than the other national sides. But in many ways it is possible to create more enthusiasm for playing for Scotland or Wales or Northern Ireland because these countries have been traditionally football underdogs and they are out to show the England team just what they can do.

Almost because of the large amount of talent at Ramsey's disposal he has to contend with a certain apathy among professional players. In an age when many youngsters would question their obligations to *fight* for their country, it is not surprising that some of them are less than enthusiastic about playing football in the national team.

We have already discussed the handling of the Todd/Hudson affair and whatever say Ramsey had in this it has certainly not enhanced his reputation as someone who is able to command the respect of younger players. Both players had been messed about by Ramsey, pulling them in and out of the England squad, and then peremptorily calling them up for an Under-23 tour. It is hardly surprising that both Hudson and Todd refused, pleading tiredness or domestic problems as the excuse, when both must have wondered whether the journey was really necessary if they could not be sure of a regular team place.*

It seems there has always been a conflict between club and country, dating back from the time when a crowded fixture list now means that clubs are involved in football from July through to the following May, often playing fifty or sixty games in that time, including visits to Europe, FA and League Cup games,

*The ban on Todd and Hudson was lifted in June 1973

minor competitions and a full League programme. It is hardly surprising that some players are complaining they have enough football.

Ramsey was apparently so out of touch with the mood of his players that a round robin was handed to him on the aeroplane coming back from Berlin to the effect that his squad were too tired or unwilling to take part in any more fixtures, with the result that a subsequent June tour was abruptly cancelled.

Chapter 12

Conclusions

The season 1972–3 will go down in football history as the year of the missing millions, the decline of attendances at League matches that started in the summer – when everyone blamed the Olympics on television – and continued through the season, reducing attendances to the lowest figure since the war.

Curiously enough everyone except the administrators seemed concerned about the decline and apart from blaming television, the newspapers or the weather little constructive comment emerged from Lancaster Gate or Lytham St Annes.

The football machine however continued to rumble on. Bert Head of Crystal Palace continued to prop up his sagging side and spent a cool £270,000 on new players. Ted McDougall, hero of Bournemouth United who a few months previously had declared 'My future is here' moved to Manchester United for £220,000, and thence to West Ham. The players' union were demanding a fee of £250 for appearance in internationals and calling for the end of the retain and transfer system – at last. By mid-season thirty-nine players had been sent off, including four on Boxing Day in the best traditions of the season of good-will. A satirical paper called *Foul* made its appearance, as 'a radical alternative to the existing football press'. *The Sunday Times* published a 'bovver guide' to First Division grounds, complete with symbols denoting 'good cops' or 'beware railway station'. Third Division Charlton had their biggest gate of the season, 7,000, leaving room at the ground for just 53,000 more. Eldon Griffiths, Minister for Sport, blamed too much television for the fall in attendances and Burnley's Bob Lord banned the cameras from his ground.

Meanwhile the dust had settled at Manchester United and George Best had been out of the news for over a week. Tommy Docherty, newly installed after the swift and merciless despatch of Frank O'Farrell, was already flexing his managerial muscles and within ten days had snapped up Arsenal's George Graham and a young Scottish defender Alex Forsyth and others, bringing United's spending on new players to over £800,000 in just ten months.

Is there then anything *wrong* with English football? There is no simple answer to this question. There is almost certainly too much football: in the week before I wrote this chapter there was a full programme of League games, European matches and knock-out competitions of one kind or another every evening except Thursday. Over the weekend viewers watched highlights of six matches on television.

This is more football than supporters can cope with, given the current promotion or lack of it applied to the game. If football persists in staging this number of fixtures something must be done about selling them to the public. No club advertises regularly and unless you catch a particular edition of the previous Saturday's evening paper you have no idea what fixtures are taking place during the coming week. Often it is not until Monday or Tuesday that you realize there are half a dozen games you could watch by scanning the small print on the sports pages, and to do that you must be already committed.

For too long clubs have relied on their captive audiences, publicising forthcoming fixtures in the club programme or by means of dreary unprofessional announcements over the public address system. This is fine for the spectators gathered there, if they are listening. But what about attracting a new football following?

Too great a reliance is placed on television. While taking most of the blame for falling attendances, the sports programmes do an excellent unpaid PR job for the industry, announcing details of fixtures and replays, and – perhaps most generously of all – heavily plugging benefit matches that would otherwise pass unnoticed in the football calendar.

Instead of biting the hands that feed them, managers and others running football should acknowledge their obligations to the press and television and start learning to be more approachable. There is an insatiable demand for football news and managers should welcome pressmen instead of regarding them as an unwarranted intrusion into their closed little world.

Certainly too the standard of overall spectator comfort must improve. More is needed than the construction of a few high-priced private boxes. There is no reason why all spectators should not be seated and under cover. The Wheatley Report on crowd safety may be a move in the right direction and bringing grounds under the control of the licensing authority will force clubs unwillingly or otherwise into closer relationship with the communities they serve.

The football administrators should also get their perspectives right. Both the League and the FA have had a lot to say about football violence, yet nothing has been done by way of research into the problem and all the evidence shows that what occurs is minimal and gets blown up by irresponsible sections of the press. Why not a counter-propaganda campaign here?

Finally the administrators must start to bring their thinking into line with the 1970s. In 1972, all of us witnessed what one man in the uncompromising shape of Avery Brundage did to the Olympic movement. And many of us marvelled at the antics of the Amateur Swimming Association is suspending some of their best performers.

As though desperate not to be outdone in stupidity, the FA senselessly clapped suspensions on two of England's brightest hopes for the 1974 World Cup with all the solemnity of an old-fashioned public hanging.

The sad thing is that no one seems to care. Next Saturday's game is already upon us and somehow we will all muddle through.